The
National
Gallery
of
Canada

Acknowledgements

This book has been written with the generous assistance of members of the staff of the National Gallery of Canada, and with the advice of Maud Brown, the widow of the first Director of the National Gallery. Numerous quotations have been made from the small book Mrs Brown wrote on her husband, aptly called *Breaking Barriers* (1964). A helpful document in examining the early history of the Gallery has been the typescript *History of the Royal Canadian Academy of Art* (1934) by Hugh G. Jones and Edmond Dyonnet. Other information comes from 'Eric Brown as I Knew Him' by W. G. Constable in *Canadian Art,* Spring 1953. For material on the first chairman of the Board, Sir Edmund Walker, I have made use of G. P. de T. Glazebrook's biography of him (Oxford University Press, 1933). I also used William Boyman Howell's book on the second chairman: *F. J. Shepherd – Surgeon: His Life and Times* (University of Toronto, 1934). The most copious quotations are from *Self Portrait* (1939) by Charles Ricketts. I am most grateful to Peter Davies Ltd, London, for permission to reproduce them. Clarke Irwin and Co. Ltd, Toronto, have kindly granted permission for quotations from Emily Carr's *Growing Pains* (1946) and A. Y. Jackson's *A Painter's Country* (1964). Other material comes from the Gallery's archives.

The National Gallery of Canada

Jean Sutherland Boggs

Toronto
OXFORD UNIVERSITY PRESS
1971

PHOTOGRAPH CREDITS

Plate XV by John Evans, Ottawa; Plate
98 by the artist, David Smith. All
other photography done by the Photographic Services Section of the National
Gallery of Canada: C. Ellis Kerr (Chief
Photographer), L. V. Cave, A. A. Wellard.

ISBN 0–19–540189–1

Photoset by Filmtype Services Ltd, Scarborough,
England
Colour and monochrome plates printed in Germany
by Boss-Druck und Verlag, Kleve
Text Printed in Germany by Herder Druck, Freiburg
Bound in Germany by Karl Hanke, Düsseldorf

Contents

Preface

It would take the talents of a Horatio Alger to capture the particular poignancy and nobility of the survival of the National Gallery of Canada while chronicling its undeniably heroic achievements. We Canadians like to apologize for our institutions because of their youth, but our National Gallery is only fifty-six years younger than London's, thirty years junior to Edinburgh's, and was established sixteen years after Dublin's. It was founded a decade after the Metropolitan Museum of Art in New York and fifty-six years before the National Gallery of Art in Washington. But it could be argued that, although it was conceived in 1880, it was actually born only in 1913, with the appointment of Trustees under a strong chairman, legislation of its own, and a Director; the thirty-three years before were a long, though perhaps historically necessary, parturition. Even after 1913, however, its history was sufficiently harsh to have invited Alger's admiration.

At no time – or certainly not until after the Second World War – was the National Gallery of Canada indulged. There have been occasional donations of works and even generous bequests of collections from the estates of Dr James M. MacCallum, Vincent Massey, and Douglas M. Duncan, but never a Maecenas (although H. S. Southam was instinctively one) to give the Gallery what it needed. The collection was assembled with the disciplined use of meagre funds (a virtue those of both Scottish and French descent in Canada could admire). Most unusually among art museums of the world, the National Gallery of Canada can be proudly claimed as the gift of the country's taxpayers. Their contribution has not been large: $154,776 for the thirty-three years from 1880 to 1913 and $7,205,793 for the fifty-five years the Gallery was incorporated independently between 1913 and 1968. It has never cost the taxpayer as much as five cents *per capita* a year.

Since this is a history of the collection – and appropriately so, because the collection is the mainspring of the Gallery's other activities – it may not become apparent that Canada's National Gallery, probably for geographic reasons, has had two claims to distinction among national art museums of the world. It has, first of all, always considered its responsibilities to be national rather than local and even by 1918 had begun to provide services and send exhibitions regularly to communities between Halifax and Vancouver. Secondly it has been particularly close to Canadian artists. Sometimes, as will be seen, that relationship has been uneasy, but it has never been indifferent. The Gallery has felt responsible to the best in Canadian art and has made every effort to make it better known at home and abroad.

The heroism of the institution and its triumph against hardships and obstacles is, of course, the sum of the heroisms of its staff, supporters, and trustees. The interests of Canadian artists have also been part of its development. And the Canadian government's Prime Ministers, Cabinet Ministers, and Members of Parliament have somehow miraculously kept this eccentric National Gallery alive.

The National Gallery is in the capital of Canada. The city of Ottawa has grown from 14,669 in 1861 to 294,377 in 1967; it has a mixed French- and English-speaking population. (The Gallery's attendance has always been surprisingly high – 484,506, for example, in 1970.) As the capital, Ottawa is, first of all, the seat of the Governor-General, the Crown's representative in Canada. One Governor-General, the Marquis of Lorne, was the founder of the National Gallery. In the fifty-five years the Gallery was incorporated independently (1913–68) every Governor-General in turn was honorary President of the Board; and at least one, Lord Willingdon, used to chair its meetings. The Governors-General, however, have inevitably been less important to the Gallery's development than Parliament and the Prime Ministers; debates in the House and the concern of succeeding Ministers and Prime Ministers are an essential part of the Gallery's history.

The somewhat unconventional collection of the National Gallery – which stands in the capital as a symbol and measure of the nation's interest in the visual arts – has been formed by the support of Governors-General, the appropriations of Parliament, the knowledge and judgement of its Directors and Trustees, the generosity of donors, and the creative activity of Canada's artists. It is true that it is small, but it is also distinguished. And it has a vitality that comes from its traditional involvement with living artists. It is a collection – it even has a history – in which Canadians should take pride.

1 1880–1907
Years of Obscurity

The first twenty-seven years of the National Gallery of Canada are almost embarrassingly obscure. There has even been some rancorous discussion about whether or not its history can be considered to have begun in 1880. To be certain, it then possessed neither legislation nor a building. But as a concept it appeared in speeches and newspaper reports and it did possess a small collection of the diploma works of the newly founded Royal Canadian Academy.

In explaining the first exhibition of the Royal Canadian Academy, which was to open on 6 March 1880, the *Ottawa Daily Citizen* reported that 'Each Academician has agreed to give a diploma picture as a condition of his appointment, to be presented to the Government, to form the nucleus of a national gallery at Ottawa, which it is to be hoped will soon become worthy of the Dominion. These pictures will be selected by His Excellency and H. R. H. the Princess, and will doubtless be the cream of the exhibition.' The *Citizen*'s confidence in the Governor-General and his wife was not misplaced; he was the Marquis of Lorne, the future Duke of Argyll, and she was Princess Louise, a daughter of Queen Victoria, who was, like her mother, a skilful painter. Both the Lornes showed a genuine interest in the arts, and it was he who undoubtedly pushed the Royal Canadian Academy and an undernourished National Gallery of Canada into being.

Lorne naturally opened the first Academy exhibition. (Princess Louise was absent because of a sleigh accident three weeks before.) At that socially important if provincially disorganized event at the Clarendon Hotel the Governor-General was reported in the *Ottawa City* as saying: 'A glance at the constitution of the society will show your objects are declared to be . . . the formation of a National Gallery at the seat of Government.' He went on to expand on the objects of the Academy, and when he came to the Gallery he said: 'With regard to the third object I have mentioned, the gentlemen who have been appointed Academicians have patriotically undertaken as a guarantee of their interest in the welfare of art in Canada, that it shall be a condition of their acceptance of the office of academician that they shall give, each of them, a picture which shall become national property, and be placed here in an art gallery.'

We can reasonably suspect that an enthusiastic Lorne had persuaded the future Academicians of their patriotic duty to support a gallery, as they had planned together for this exhibition and for the constitution of the society. He and Princess Louise made a point of visiting the 1882 exhibition of the Royal Canadian Academy in Ottawa on the first day it was held, in space considered to be the Gallery's own. Lorne gave some Canadian sculpture to the collection and two wooden statuettes that he believed to be sixteenth-century, and he and Princess Louise persuaded three English Academicians – Leighton (plate 79), Millais (plate 80), and Watts (plate 81) – to make contributions to this new National Gallery in Canada. The year after they returned to England, Princess Louise sent a competent portrait she herself had painted.

The Lornes' enthusiasm fell on decidedly barren ground. Their interest in stimulating and supporting a National Gallery does not, unhappily, seem to have been shared by subsequent Governors-General within the first twenty-seven years of its history. Nevertheless a Privy Council decision of 29 March 1880 'advised that the diploma pictures presented to the National Gallery by the Canadian Academy be placed under the care of the Minister of Public Works'. More specifically the Gallery came under the office of the Chief Architect.

Neither the Ministry nor the Chief Architect provided it with distinguished surroundings. Its first permanent home was in remodelled builders' workshops on Parliament Hill that it shared with the Supreme Court; it was given a single room of 36 × 20 feet that was opened to the public on 27 May 1882. As the *Ottawa Citizen* commented in 1886: 'the halls of the Supreme Court, however well they may echo the sonorous voices of the ermine-clad sages (who by the way have been worked up to a fine frenzy by the ruthless invasion of their domain), are not adapted to the showing of pictures.'

The Supreme Court may have contributed to the move in 1888 from Parliament Hill to rooms above the Government Fisheries exhibit on O'Connor Street. The *Ottawa Daily Free Press* of 10 March 1888 commented: 'In more ways than one the change is advantageous; in two, particularly so. The whole collection is now in one room with ample hanging space for it at present, and being alongside the better-known and more popular fisheries exhibit is likely to receive a greater amount of attention from visitors than has hitherto fallen to its lot.' The attendance did go up: from 11,943 in the old building in 1886–7 to a peak of 22,961 visitors in 1895–6; but then began a steady decline, which may have added to the government's concern when it was persuaded by the Academy to consider the state of the Gallery in 1907.

The Royal Canadian Academy was the Gallery's principal patron during these early years. When its first Act was passed in 1882 it moved the Gallery up from the third object in Lorne's 1880 speech to 'First – the institution of a National Gallery at the seat of government'. It had already made a contribution by a deposit of diploma works, some as fine as the painting of its first president, Lucius O'Brien, whose *Sunrise on the Saguenay* we have reproduced in colour (plate XXII). Naturally not all the diploma works could be of uniform quality, but by 1891 the Gallery had acquired through the Academicians a collection of good nineteenth-century Canadian paintings, including works by Hamel, Homer Watson (plate 112), Plamondon (plate 111), Robert Harris, Jacobi, Brymner (plate 113), Bell-Smith, William Raphael, and George Reid. Of these only two could be considered as in any way pandering to sentimental Victorian taste: Harris's *Chorister* and Reid's *Mortgaging the Homestead* (plate 116); but both are interesting as works by otherwise serious, responsible painters. The most enchanting diploma work was by the first Vice-President, Napoléon Bourassa, and is called *Légende du berceau: l'enfant sourit aux anges*; since he was both a church muralist and a caricaturist, it seems inpossible to gauge its seriousness. In addition, between 1890 and 1894 the R.C.A. did buy for the Gallery some works from its own exhibitions and the World's Columbian Exposition of 1893 in Chicago.

The Academy must have played a further role in relation to the Gallery but this is difficult to assess. Nothing suggests a particular interest on the part of succeeding presidents during these years: O'Brien until 1890; Otto R. Jacobi from 1890 to 1893; Robert Harris from 1893 to 1906. The only president who is known to have been active was George Reid. Born in Ontario, Reid had studied with Robert Harris and then with Thomas Eakins who encouraged him to go to Paris; he therefore knew both the United States and Europe. A typescript *History of the Royal Canadian Academy of Arts* (1934) by Hugh G. Jones and Edmond Dyonnet in which Dyonnet, secretary of the R.C.A. from 1910 to 1947, wisely disclaims any responsibility for errors, states that: 'In 1908 [actually it was 1906] Reid, newly elected president of the Academy, made a general survey of the Gallery and reported "finding the management 'very slip shod' and the custodian Watts [it must have been Walter R. Billings, Acting Curator; Watts seems to have departed by 1897] without any authority for its control".' Reid acted with dispatch. He arranged for a semi-annual meeting of the R.C.A. Council in Ottawa and worked out a draft memorial to the Governor-General, pressing 'the view of the importance and usefulness of an energetically administered National Gallery'. His achievements will be considered in the next chapter.

The Academy must have been involved in the appointment of the Gallery's first curator, John W. H. Watts, an English-born architect who was an Academician living in Ottawa. In 1882 he received a joint appointment as the Gallery's Curator (which he was called in official documents from 1883) and Assistant Chief Government Architect. The writer of an article in the *Ottawa Daily Free Press* of 10 March 1888, describing the Gallery in its new home in the Government Fisheries Building, tells of mounting the stairs lined with architectural drawings: 'They are all well hung, but that exquisite piece of pen work by Watts, "A Design for a Staircase", should be put where a closer view could be had of it.' We gather that Watts, though a modest man, had his friends in the press.

It was probably Watts (though it may have been O'Brien as the Academy's President) who in 1886 persuaded the government to make its first purchases. These were two solid pieces of genre painting from an R.C.A. exhibition: the *Crazy Patchwork* by Brymner and the *School Trustees* by Robert Harris, which is still one of the Gallery public's favourites. The government's subsequent buying was rather desultory.

In 1894 there were some signs of life. The R.C.A. made four purchases for the Gallery and Colonel H.D. Warren of Toronto gave a collection of Cypriot coins, pottery and antiquities. Finally, the government bought three works: one by the Canadian J.M. Barnsley, and the other two by living foreign artists, the Dutchmen Willem Tholen and J.H. Weissenbruch. We have no clue why the works of two foreign artists were acquired; they did, however, belong to a school of painting, the Hague School, that was receiving generous patronage in Montreal. The Tholen, which is dated 1892, had been bought in Montreal from Wm. Scott & Sons, the chief purveyor of such pictures to rich Montrealers. The next year there was another significant departure – the acquisition of the work of a Canadian artist who had died but had achieved considerable success abroad. This was Paul Peel, whose *Venetian Bather* (plate 115) was bought for the then handsome sum of $600; it had been shown at the Paris Salon in 1889 and at the Chicago World's Columbian Exposition in 1893.

It is difficult to assess the first Curator's role in the Gallery's history. Watts's reports are so impersonal and uninformative that we are apt to suspect that his may have been just another job for someone in the Chief Architect's office. In 1897 he went into private practice, and if he kept an eye on the Gallery for the R.C.A., it was, as far as the government was concerned, unofficial.

Watts's successor, L. Fennings Taylor, appears in the reports in 1897 without any fanfare whatsoever; we know only that he was not an Academician. After four years without making any purchases for the Gallery he comes to life in his annual report of 12 December 1900:

I beg to call your attention to the crowded condition of the Gallery, and the method of heating. It is impossible to hang the pictures with any degree of satisfaction on account of the lack of space. An extension at the rear or at the side of the present building could be built which would prove most acceptable and be by no means extravagant. The building is heated by a stove; a hot water apparatus would be a great improvement in cleanliness, convenience and appearance.

Taylor did get $500 the next year to buy an oil painting by Charles Huot, a contemporary Canadian, and, more interestingly, $700 the following year to buy the first Canadian work by an artist who was no longer living: *The Studio* by Krieghoff. Gradually the budget increased but so did the pressures to buy from Canadian agents for political rather than artistic reasons.

In 1907, under an Acting Curator, Walter R. Billings, the Gallery patriotically bought portraits of Edward VII and Alexandra for $5,000. But more important was its acquisition of the first work by an old master. It was a highly respectable purchase: Gainsborough's *Portrait of Ignatius Sancho* of 1768 (plate 69), which was bought at Wm. Scott & Sons, Montreal, for $2,850, with a painting by the contemporary Frenchman François Flemeng thrown in. In lecturing on the Gallery's collection in the twenties, its first director, Eric Brown, spoke of this portrait of 'a Negro who wrote verse and poetry . . . about which history records that it was painted in an hour and a half – a marvellous performance judging by the care and precision of the painting'. *Ignatius Sancho* marked a change in the Gallery's fortunes and collection.

2 1907–1913
A Beginning

The purchase of the Gainsborough introduced a new period in the history of the Gallery. Spearheaded by George Reid, President of the Royal Canadian Academy, serious consideration was given for the first time to the Gallery's function, housing, and administration, as well as to its acquisitions.

In a memorial conveyed through the Governor-General to the government, Reid and the Academy offered a solution for a stronger national museum of art: 'an advisory council of laymen, a co-operating committee of artists appointed by the Academy, adequate appropriations, and a competent full-time director'. Fortunately both the Minister of Public Works, Sidney Fisher, and the Governor-General offered their support. But the Governor-General, Lord Grey, was also interested in freeing the Gallery from the control of the Academy and wrote to Reid about 'the possibility of too much control by the proposed co-operating artists committee'. In return the Academy 'communicated its decision that it would not seek representation on the Advisory Council, but would make its representations to the body as occasion arose'.

As a result a government minute of 3 April 1907 established this council, stating that 'such a Council should be composed by gentlemen who have shown their interest in an appreciation and understanding of art as evidenced by their public connection with art associations and their private patronage of art'. The government appointed three laymen: Sir George Drummond, Montreal businessman and collector; Mr Byron E. (later Sir Edmund) Walker, Toronto businessman; and Senator Arthur Boyer from Montreal. Thus a precedent was established for appointing to the council or board of the Gallery members who were from Canadian communities other than Ottawa and had ties with other Canadian museums (in Drummond's case the Art Association of Montreal, now the Montreal Museum of Fine Arts;

in Walker's the Toronto Art Museum, now the Art Gallery of Ontario, and the Royal Ontario Museum).

It must be admitted that this Council did not become a decisive instrument until the death of Drummond in 1910 and his replacement as chairman by Walker, of whom the Academy's history records: 'Sir Edmund seems to have been a strong man with a liking for his own way of doing things.' Drummond's place on the Council was taken by Dr Francis J. Shepherd of Montreal. In a private letter many years later, the first Director of the Gallery, Eric Brown, confided: 'Sir Edmund always showed good taste and judgement in practically everything that was bought for the National Gallery collection, whether Canadian or foreign. Dr Shepherd was really only interested in the continental French Barbizon and contemporary Dutch schools, while Boyer was interested in practically nothing. So gradually the collection was built up with minor opposition and a good deal of help from Dr Shepherd and some actual, though not strong opposition, from Mr Boyer.'

One occasion Boyer rebelled was when the Gallery acquired its first work by Horatio Walker, a Canadian painter of Millet-inspired subjects from the Québec countryside who had achieved a considerable reputation in Europe and New York and whose prices were among the highest of any artist of his generation (far higher, for example, at that moment than Van Gogh's or Gauguin's). Sir Edmund worriedly discussed the problem in a letter of 9 December 1910 to the Minister of Public Works. He wrote of 'the necessity that we should possess an example of the work of Horatio Walker before opening the National Gallery to the Canadian public' in the newly constructed building to be known as the Victoria Museum. The Council had concluded that 'his pictures brought very high prices' and, after having met in New York and considered some for as much as $15,000 and $17,000, had settled on the *Oxen Drinking* (plate 118) for $10,000. Walker went on to point out that, although the artist was 'of course no relation to me in any way', he owned an oil by him for which he had paid $6,000 and a watercolour that had cost $1,500, and added: 'I am personally quite sure that the price is right, so much so that I should be prepared to take it out of the hands of the Government if any sound criticism could be raised against its purchase.'

After the New York visit Boyer changed his mind and decided to question the price of the work and withhold his approval of its purchase. In writing to the Minister, Walker pointed out that 'if this were a question of the purchase of a picture painted by an artist other than a Canadian I should not urge its purchase with one member dissenting'. But urge he did and, in spite of Boyer's dissenting vote, it now hangs in the National Gallery. Judgement about whether the Senator or Sir Edmund was right will probably vary from generation to generation. Horatio Walker seems more interesting to us now than he did a generation ago, and in 1970 the Gallery acquired its fourth oil by him, for little more than one third the 1910 price.

The Council was also given, as the Academy had hoped, regular appropriations. A government minute of 3 April 1907 stated that 'the expenditure of the various sums of money is entrusted to the Minister of Public Works and it is important that such money should be spent to the best advantage in securing for the country objects of rare value from the artistic standpoint and in promoting growth and true taste and general interest in public Art among the people of Canada.' The Council was able to control the Ministry's expenditure of such funds. Though these 'sums of money' were perhaps not as adequate as the Academy had wished, they established the principle of regular government appropriations for the National Gallery. From its annual grant of $10,000, the Gallery dutifully spent $4,060 for eleven works from the 1908 R.C.A. exhibition and the next year bought sixty-eight works from the Academy. When in 1911 Walker helped bring down Sir Wilfrid Laurier's government in opposition to its measure for trade reciprocity with the United States, he could write confidently to another member of the Gallery's Council: 'I feel we shall get things done now.' It was not until 1913, however, that the National Gallery's grant for all its activities reached $100,000 a year.

The last of the Academy's aims – a competent full-time Director – was achieved in 1910. He was a thirty-three-year-old Englishman, Eric Brown, whom Walker had met in the old Art Association of Montreal building on Phillips Square. When Brown was asked to make a report to the trustees after twenty years at the Gallery, he described the institution as he had found it:

In 1910, when I was appointed Curator [as he was called for a year], *the National Gallery of Canada, although having been established for thirty years, that is since 1880, still occupied a small and dingy upstairs gallery on O'Connor St above the Fisheries Exhibition. The collection consisted of the diploma pictures of the R.C.A., one or two purchases made in 1909 by the newly appointed Advisory Arts Council and a number of other acquisitions by gift or purchase, none of them important and most of them frankly detrimental to any art collection and acquired by means that are better left unexplored. No records of any kind were available . . . except two or three incomplete catalogues published since 1880.*

Brown was to remain as Director until his death twenty-nine years later.

Walker would go on buying trips himself – he did not leave purchasing in the hands of his Acting Curator, Mr Billings, nor even later with Eric Brown. He had a deep interest in Canadian art. It is revealing that in these years before the official establishment of the Gallery with its own Act and Board in 1913, among the Homer Watsons, Brymners, and Brownells that the Gallery had always bought, there were now acquisitions by other artists – all of them working in, or from, Québec, and all having close links with France: Maurice Cullen (plate 122), Clarence Gagnon, and James Wilson Morrice, one of Canada's most subtle painters. His *Quai des Grands-Augustins, Paris* (plate 120) was bought in 1909. That same year Gagnon's *Rue du Canal, Moret sur Loing*, and twenty-one of his etchings, were purchased from the artist. Although not the first prints in the Gallery's collection, the Gagnons could be regarded as the first conscious expression of an interest in prints and drawings that resulted in Canada's largest print room. In appointing Brown, Sir Edmund found a willing disciple who was ready to share his enthusiasm for the work of Canadian artists and also for prints and drawings.

Walker and Brown made the real beginnings of the European collection – bought with very little money but with a fundamental desire to give Canadians a sense of history. While Walker was founding this traditional collection of European painting, he was also working with Charles Currelly on Canada's great archaeological collection in the Royal Ontario Museum, Toronto, and had drafted a letter to the Premier of Ontario stressing, among other things, 'the value of the education of people through seeing objects which are interesting archaeologically, artistically, scientifically or for individual or economic reasons'. When in 1912 Currelly let Ottawa have a Fayum portrait for the price he had paid for it earlier that year at auction in London, Brown shared Walker's pride in the small panel as the beginning of a 'chronological survey' through the collection.

By 1913 Walker and Brown, working together in great sympathy and harmony, could claim that the Gallery now represented: Venice in the fifteenth century; Florence, Flanders, and Germany in the sixteenth; Rome, Flanders, Spain, and Holland in the seventeenth; and England and France in the eighteenth. In the speeches custom requires of the Director of the National Gallery, Eric Brown was able to describe the collection in these terms:

Of Primitive Italian pictures there is a fine full-length picture called 'The Saviour' attributed to Cima de Conegliano [plate 9], a small Madonna by Marco Bello, pupil and friend of Giovanni Bellini, and as showing the primitive influence on the Dutchmen there is a brilliant Frans Floris, figures in landscape, full of lustrous colour and quaint charm. All these pictures are typical of their time and ideals. Their colour is pure and strong and in a wonderful way the emotional endeavour to realize their subject has overcome their technical limitations.

There is a fine Caravaggio 'Portrait of a Cardinal' [plate 19] showing the tremendous power of directness with which that unfettered individuality was to create a new age in painting.

The attributions of many of these pictures so lovingly bought with modest funds have changed. The 'Cima' over the years has been given somewhat unconvincingly by the most knowing scholars – Berenson, Hendy, and Kenneth Clark – to Giovanni Bellini. The 'Caravaggio' has just recently been established as the only painting in North America by the seventeenth-century Bolognese painter, Andrea Sacchi. These purchases – which also included a Domenico Puligo, a Hogarth (plate 67), and a Reynolds (plate 68) – did represent 'their time and ideals' and did reveal, as Brown was aware, certain 'limitations' as works bought for a historical interest (which has survived) on a budget that averaged slightly over $20,000 a year.

Of this transitional period, which was to come to an end with an Act for the Gallery in 1913, Eric Brown was able quite accurately to say that, though the Gallery had had a short active life, 'much has been accomplished, and with greater facilities in the shape of more room and greater freedom of management [it] will accomplish worthily its task of fostering and advancing the national art of Canada and of educating its people to some understanding of the world's artistic achievement'.

3 1913–1924
Walker and the Heroic Years

In 1913 the National Gallery of Canada was finally given its own Act, which embodied the convictions stated in the creation of the Advisory Arts Council in 1907 and which had been expressed in the speeches of the Director after his appointment in 1910. Behind this legislation was the genuine and unrelenting patriotism of the first Chairman of the Board of Trustees, Sir Edmund Walker.

Sir Edmund saw the Act through its drafting and into the House. Again there was a reason for Walker to be a 'strong man', for the Royal Canadian Academy was drafting new legislation at the same time. As he wrote to the Director on 15 January 1913: 'I was extremely angry to find a section in a bill about to be introduced by the Royal Canadian Academy . . . which seemed to indicate a desire on their part to exercise some control over the National Gallery.' The Academy's history states: 'Sir Edmund absolutely and positively refused both acknowledgment of parentage and representation of the Academy in the new National Gallery – he wouldn't even discuss it.' Finally a compromise was suggested in which the Academy's role was 'to continue to aid in the advancement of the National Gallery'. The history concludes: 'For the Academy agreement could not have been more than a gesture of obeisance to power in the hands of Chairman and Minister.'

Sir Edmund was quite ready to put what power he possessed at the disposal of the Gallery's interests – particularly in defending its freedom from any pressure groups. The clarity with which he saw the issues and potential dangers in drafting legislation for the Gallery, and in implementing it, was also characteristic of his interest in other Canadian institutions. One of these was the Canadian Bank of Commerce, of which he was Chief Executive Officer from 1886 and President from 1907 until his retirement in 1915. A second was the University of Toronto; he was chairman of its Board of

Governors from 1910. Another was the Toronto museum now known as the Art Gallery of Ontario; from 1900 he was Chairman of the provisionary committee that raised money and brought it into being. When it finally opened on its present site in 1918 Walker was President of its Board. His real passion, however, was the Royal Ontario Museum, for which he worked from 1905 with its first Director, Charles Currelly; they had been students together at Victoria University (now part of the University of Toronto) and had taken Saturday painting classes from Lucius O'Brien. Currelly, in his autobiography *I Brought the Ages Home*, recorded that in 1909 Walker 'was so much excited by the possibilities of the Chinese collection that he offered to back me for twenty thousand at the bank which, with the grant of ten thousand, gave me a working capital of thirty thousand'. In 1912 Walker became the first Chairman of the Board of this museum, which opened officially two years later. He was doing all of this and more while he worked with Eric Brown on the National Gallery of Canada.

Walker had been able to get a building for the Art Museum of Toronto and the Royal Ontario Museum but he was not successful in obtaining one for the National Gallery. Nevertheless, in 1912 the Gallery had moved out of the Fisheries Building into accommodation provided, along with space for the National Museum (of natural history and anthropology), in the Victoria Museum. But even then the Gallery could not settle down. When fire destroyed part of the Parliament Buildings in 1916, Parliament took over the space occupied by the Gallery and the museums. The collection had to go into storage until the legislators departed in 1921. 'Parliament has gone back to its home on the hill,' Eric Brown wrote then; 'the National Gallery is open again to everyone's joy.' And he went on: 'There is no hiding the fact that the present premises of the National Gallery, in the east wing of the Victoria Museum, are makeshift ones, and if a National Gallery building was started tomorrow, it could not be finished a moment too soon to supply the need, because the galleries are absolutely filled to over-flowing and there is no room whatever for any expansion.' Discouragingly it was to be almost another forty years before the Gallery moved, and even then the move was to temporary quarters.

The financial history of the Gallery was equally erratic. In 1913, in its enthusiasm for the new legislation, the government gave the Gallery an annual grant of $100,000 for all its expenses; but on 3 November 1914, after the outbreak of war, this patriotic resolution appeared in the Board's minutes: 'In view of the abnormal condition of affairs consequent upon the European war it was resolved that the Trustees should recommend to the Government the cutting down of the National Gallery appropriation for 1915–16 from $100,000 to $25,000.' Before the war was over the appropriation was to fall even further and only managed to climb up again to $100,000 in the fiscal year 1923–4, just before Walker's death. The Trustees believed in spending this money where it would endure. Of the $100,000 they had in 1913–14 for the Gallery, $88,500 was spent on acquisitions.

Walker's patriotism in asking that the Gallery's appropriations be reduced in wartime was not an isolated incident. It helps explain his devotion to a group of artists that he felt had produced a truly national school of painting: these were Tom Thomson and the Group of Seven – Franklin Carmichael, Lawren Harris, A. Y. Jackson, Frank Johnston, Arthur Lismer, J. E. H. MacDonald, and Frederick H. Varley. A. Y. Jackson, in *A Painter's Country*, describes the Group's early contact with the Gallery:

We were inclined to be very vocal about our ideas. Harris and I wrote letters to the papers, criticizing the National Gallery for its neglect of Canadian art. We expected to be black-listed by the Gallery for our effrontery; instead of that, Sir Edmund Walker, who was Chairman of the Board of Trustees, came around to see Harris and asked to know what all the fuss was about. Harris told him of our intention to paint our own country and to put life into Canadian art. Sir Edmund said that was just what the National Gallery wanted to see happen; if it did, the Gallery would back us up. The Gallery was as good as its word.

Eric Brown echoed Walker's commitment in a speech during the war:

There is no doubt that the most significant thing about Canadian art today is its group of younger landscape painters. . . . From a centre which may be said to be in a certain studio building in Toronto . . . these apostles of the decorative landscape have gone forth into the wilds of Canadian nature and have found a veritable wonderland which holds them enthralled. In their decorative arrangement and brilliant colour one sees the hope of a distinctly national school of landscape painting which at present seems more allied to the modern Scandinavian than to anything the United Kingdom has produced.

The Gallery's first purchases of Group painting were gentle landscapes by Lawren Harris and J. E. H. MacDonald in 1912. The first canvas in the Gallery's collection to represent the direction the Group would take was A. Y. Jackson's *The Red Maple* (plate 127), bought from a Royal Canadian Academy exhibition for $500 in 1914, the same year the first paintings by Lismer and Tom Thomson were acquired. Eric Brown described it as 'a blood red maple tree silhouetted against the blue and brown of a rushing stream'. The next year

Thomson's *Northern River* was added, and the year after his *Spring Ice* for $300; with his death his chief patron, Dr J. M. MacCallum, persuaded the Gallery to buy the *Jack Pine* (plate XXVIII) and twenty-five of his small oil sketches. The support was not evenly divided among the members of the Group, however – works by Carmichael and Varley were not bought until 1921 – but by the time Walker died in March 1924 the Gallery had four Harrises, seven Jacksons, five Franz Johnstons, five Lismers, eight Mac-Donalds, two Varleys, and one Carmichael in its collection.

Walker and Brown were constantly put on the defensive because of their sponsorship of this small group of Canadian artists. The Academy was highly critical of the Gallery's favouritism in selecting Canadian works for purchase or to be exhibited abroad. This seems to have reached a peak in 1924, just before Walker's death, when the Gallery was asked by the government to organize the Canadian participation in an Empire exhibition to be held at Wembley in London. The Academy's history tells us: 'The Academy immediately protested that the Gallery, as a museum directed by laymen, was not fairly representative of the artists of Canada. Further the Academy maintained the direction of the Gallery had over a period of years displayed such marked preference for the work of a claimed-to-be new Canadian school of painting that selection by it could not very well result in other than a showing unrepresentative of the best in all phases of Canadian art.' To appease the Academy the jury for both Wembley exhibitions (there was another in 1925) was made up of Academicians, with Eric Brown given a determining vote in the case of a tie. As it happened, Thomson and the Group of Seven aroused great interest among the critics in England, which no doubt helps to explain what the Academy history describes as the 'growing antagonism' between the Academy and the Gallery.

The acquisition of non-Canadian art in the eleven years between the legislation and Walker's death was modest – probably because of the reduction in appropriations; the purchase budget averaged about $35,000 a year.

Acquisitions that suggest Sir Edmund's influence were three fourteenth-century Florentine panels with gold backgrounds, bought in 1922–3: a *Madonna and Child* attributed to Taddeo Gaddi, *Three Saints* attributed to Agnolo Gaddi, and *Saint John the Evangelist* by 'a Friend of Pietro Lorenzetti'. As early as 1894 Sir Edmund had given a lecture at the University of Toronto on 'Early Italian Painters', which he began by asking his audience to become 'Italians of the thirteenth century for the moment'. Among the most successful purchases were two portraits of a woman (plate 7) and a man, by Bartel Bruyn, bought in 1913. Walker's interests can also be seen in the desire to expand the collection – first with the acquisition in 1913 of a Chinese painting, which Brown explained was intended 'to draw the trail across to the east', and with the purchase in 1922 of two Assyrian reliefs of Assurnasir-pal.

For us today the most admirable purchases seem to have been made in two areas: nineteenth-century French painting, and prints and drawings. A historically important painting by a favourite artist of the period was bought in New York in 1914; this was the *Oedipus* (plate 44) by Millet, which had been exhibited at the Paris Salon of 1845. In the same city and the same year, the Gallery acquired from Durand-Ruel the *Waterloo Bridge* (plate 49) by Monet and the *Washerwomen near Champagne* by Sisley. After the war it returned to New York for a large and fierce pastel by Degas, his *Danseuses à la barre* (plate 55), and the *Le pont de pierre à Rouen* (plate 48) by Pissarro. No additions were made to this part of the collection until after the Second World War. (It is interesting to note that the Gallery's source for foreign works was now New York.)

Walker, who himself collected prints, was intent upon establishing a Print Room. In 1913 a group of prints – including works by Dürer, Rembrandt, and Goltzius – was bought from Gutekunst in London. At the meeting of 15 December 1913 'It was resolved that the Trustees, in order to improve the collection of prints, should as occasion required ask Mr R. Gutekunst to make purchases for the National Gallery at the best prices obtainable.' The war interrupted this project, but in 1921 the Gallery proudly appointed its first curator of prints, H. P. Rossiter, a Canadian veteran who had worked in the Print Room at the Museum of Fine Arts, Boston. When the Gallery collection was taken out of storage and returned to the Victoria Museum in 1921, the Trustees were pleased with their four print galleries, to which Rossiter had already made important contributions, including a number of fine Dürers and proof impressions of Blake's *Job*. By early 1923 it was clear that Rossiter was going to be lost because Boston was asking him to return at a higher salary. Walker wrote in his journal on 14 January 1923: 'I made it clear that if the Civil Service Commission made it impossible for us to pay the modest salary required by Rossiter, we would be prevented from having any print expert and they would be responsible for such a state of affairs and not the trustees. . . . I have done my best but I have not much hope. The government is losing all its expert ability through failure to meet conditions as they exist.' Finally in November Rossiter's resignation was sadly accepted.

Even before Rossiter was appointed, a collection of drawings was begun. In 1911, at Gimpel & Wildenstein in New York, the Council had bought a group of seventeen Old Master drawings from the Duke of Rutland's collection; among them was the *Lute Player* (plate 162) by Annibale Carracci. The next year they bought fifteen Barbizon drawings from Cottier, again in New York, and in 1914 Daumier's *Three Judges at a Hearing* (plate 172) from Wm. Scott & Sons, Montreal. Rossiter's own triumphant and perhaps last acquisitions for the Gallery appear to have been four Goyas (including plates 168 and 169) from a Bordeaux sketchbook. They were bought, with another drawing attributed to Goya, from Colnaghi in 1923.

In 1917 Lord Beaverbrook had formed a committee to sponsor a visual record of the Canadian participation in the First World War. Money was raised and paintings were commissioned from English artists. Walker pointed out that no attention was being paid to the war effort in Canada or to Canadian artists. As a result four painters – C. W. Beatty, Maurice Cullen, F. W. Simpson, and F. H. Varley (plate 130) – were given honorary commissions and sent overseas to paint; and others, such as A. Y. Jackson (plate 128) and David Milne, found serving in the ranks, were seconded for service as war artists. Walker was, as we would have expected, very much involved in this enterprise and became a member of the Canadian War Memorials Committee.

The War Memorials were exhibited in Montreal and Toronto in 1919 and 1920 before being shown in Ottawa when the Gallery opened again in 1921. Eric Brown reviewed the second Toronto showing and was clearly ill at ease with its modernity. Even watercolours of the western front by David Milne, the only Canadian in the New York Armory Show of 1913, presented problems to Brown: 'His latest method leaves out all superfluities and when you can get rid of the idea that the white uncovered paper represents snow you begin to grasp his meaning.' He was bothered by the 'acute angles' of Bomberg's *Sappers at Work* and found Paul Nash's *Night Bombardment* 'solid and static', while admitting it moved young painters 'to panegyrics – so perhaps it is a question of growth'. Out of the accident of the First World War and Lord Beaverbrook's interest in securing a record of it, the National Gallery acquired an important group of early twentieth-century English paintings, including Harold Gilman's *Halifax Harbour at Sunset* (plate 87), Wyndham Lewis's *A Canadian Gun-pit*, Paul Nash's *Void* (plate 88), William Roberts's *The First German Gas Attack at Ypres*, and Edward Wadsworth's *Dazzle Ships* (plate 89).

The Canadian War Memorials were deposited at the Gallery in 1921. As well as paintings of the First World War by English and Canadian artists, this collection included four other pictures of great historic importance to Canadians. These were: West's *The Death of Wolfe* (plate XVII), given by the Duke of Westminster in 1918; Romney's portrait of the chief of the Six Nations Indians, *Joseph Brant* (plate 71), which Lord Beaverbrook had bought at Walker's suggestion at a Christie's auction in 1918; a portrait, attributed to Sir Thomas Lawrence, of the first white man to cross the Canadian Rockies and reach the Pacific, Sir Alexander Mackenzie; and Reynolds's *Lord Amherst*.

The period 1913 to 1924 was not easy, and yet Walker and Brown together achieved a great deal. In 1921–2 there were over 100,000 visitors to the Gallery – the Trustees were proud that it was the first museum in the country to be open on Sundays – and 200 pictures were out on loan. Walker, as a dissident Liberal who had swung to the Conservatives in 1911, was now in Brown's words 'emphatically politically *persona non grata*' with the Liberal government of Mackenzie King, which came to power in 1921; the number of Trustees was therefore increased to reduce Walker's influence. But Walker had left his indelible mark on the National Gallery out of a conviction stated (presumably by Brown) in the *Annual Report* for 1921–2 that 'Canadian education, like education everywhere, requires a close study of art at all times, because art is closely interwoven with the history of nations and the geography of countries and the story of its growth is the story of the growth of all that is intellectual and moral.' In working toward this end, the white-bearded old gentleman had collaborated so closely with elegant, monacled Eric Brown that Maud Brown could write: 'In some cases one could not tell where a new idea had originated. It unfolded spontaneously in an atmosphere of harmony and delight in their enterprises.' Walker's heirs, in his memory, gave the Gallery a portrait by Perronneau, which he would have appreciated as the first eighteenth-century French work of distinction to enter the collection.

4 1924–1931
Charles Ricketts and Brown

Another period in the history of the Gallery began with the appointment of Charles Ricketts as adviser in 1924 and ended with his death in 1931. Ricketts – not the dandelion-haired young man of the 1890s but a substantial, greying man in his sixties – advised the Gallery while it was under three Chairmen: Walker (of whom Ricketts wrote to Brown on 17 November 1923: 'I remember Sir E. Walker with pleasure, he struck me as a man of real experience and artistic judgement'); Dr F. J. Shepherd, who died in 1929; and H. S. Southam.

The choice of Ricketts as adviser had undoubtedly been Brown's, even if it was approved by Walker. Over the years Brown had advised the Gallery to buy English pictures whose value we might (perhaps quite wrongly) question today. It was presumably he who was responsible for the acquisition of two circular paintings by Ricketts' friend, Charles Shannon: the contrived portrait of Constance Collier in 1913 and that of Princess Patricia of Connaught, purchased for the Canadian War Memorials in 1919. A large painting by Ricketts himself, *The Danaids*, was added in 1922 and proudly published by Brown in *The Studio* the following year.

It seems that Ricketts came to Canada only once – in October 1927. He wrote a friend: 'I found Canada a very beautiful country, well wooded, with picturesque hills, lakes, and noble rivers, a touch of Scotland but more spacious.' On one trip into the Québec countryside across the river from Ottawa he was taken to the cottage of the Assistant Director, H. O. McCurry, at Kingsmere. He wrote about the expedition to his almost inseparable friend, Charles Shannon: 'We had tea at the cottage of the keeper of the Museum. . . . I liked his old mother-in-law [Mrs Jenkins, the sister of the poet, Archibald Lampman], who adores music, and the interior of the wooden house is all white-washed beams and timbers, rather like a Tudor interior. I was shown a genuine Indian canoe made of bark and fibre which they used on the small lake.' He described the barbershop of the Château Laurier as 'one of the vaults of Caligula's palace', and a visit to Government House: 'I was taken there in a glittering car all ebony and rock crystal, ushered in by flunkeys like Roman Emperors, and plunged into the first act of a west-end play, with beautiful young men covered with Orders, with blue silk facings to their coats (Order of St Patrick uniform). I felt I looked like Robinson Crusoe fresh from his Island.' He was delighted to learn that both the Governor-General and his wife (Lord and Lady Willingdon) were descended from Lady Dacre, whose portrait by Eworth (plate IX) he had persuaded the Gallery to buy in 1925.

Ricketts had much to recommend him as an agent for Ottawa. In 1915 he had turned down the directorship of the National Gallery, London, a decision he came to regret. On 19 June 1916 he wrote:

Found myself still haunted by refusal of the National Gallery, though this happened eight months ago and made but little impression on me at the time. I now realize that I lacked courage, insight, and public feeling, and crossed my hands when a good example there might have given tone to the art feeling of our time. It would have been a fine end to my life to nurse the dear old place; to put the Italians on whitewash or grey walls, reframe them in the gold and azure of their period, to use the dimly polished walnut at times for subsidiary frames of drawings; to place the Venetians on brocade . . . to efface the trade stencilling of the ceilings, and to slowly remould the place from a Board of Works aspect to that of a palace.

The particular talents of Ricketts were not fully used by the National Gallery of Canada. He had, for example, a superb feeling for the decoration of his environment in the tradition of Whistler and the Art Nouveau. On 20 December 1926 he wrote to Brown: 'Mr [Vincent] Massey called. I hope I did not jaw his head off. I spoke warmly about the Tintoretto portrait [plate 16], & I think convinced him of the desirability of adding good furniture to the gallery, a matter I have often gassed about to you. Durlacher actually at the moment have two good Renaissance tables & a good cassone & almost every day Christies sells superb pieces for moderate prices if they are not English or French 18th century.' We can only regret now that Ricketts was not given, say, $10,000 a year to spend on furniture. His tastes were broad. Like Whistler and Sir Edmund Walker, he appreciated the art of the Far East. And even in 1920 he was knowledgeably buying for himself a Benin head and discussing other primitive art. For the Gallery, however, he worked within a narrower tradition of European painting.

Unhappily Ricketts also had certain limitations. It would have been interesting if he had bought for the Gallery works by the nineteenth-century French painters he particularly loved, Gustave Moreau and Puvis de Chavannes. He had violent prejudices against the painters who have become most popular. On 3 November 1921 he wrote to Sydney Cockerell:

Curiously enough, I would exempt three of these men, whom the Americans found most guilty: Renoir, who is a very vulgar sensualist with a genuine painter's temperament before he became a paralytic; Toulouse-Lautrec, who is a caricaturist and satirist; and Gauguin, who had flashes of real lyrical feeling and artistic originality in a welter of haste, bad taste, and occasional incompetence. All of these men, Gauguin and Monet excepted, were physically deficient: Van Gogh a lunatic, Cézanne mentally deficient. It is a sad world.

This attitude unfortunately only encouraged Brown's own conservatism in buying. Although he made a special plea for tolerance in a letter to the *Ottawa Evening Journal* on 13 March 1926 and pointed out that the history of the past is 'very generally a story of a series of violences offered to new movements followed by their tolerance and final acceptance', Brown seems to have been opposed to the Post-Impressionists, to Cézanne, to Cubism, and to the group under which he tended to embrace all he opposed – the Futurists. 'Any movement tending to distort art and art's creation', Brown said in Vancouver on 21 June 1921, 'has as much relation to true art as Bolshevism has to true government, and candidly it is a sign of degeneracy.'

Thirty years later it is somewhat difficult to define the relationship of these men as they worked to build up the collection – communicating by letter or cable except when Brown made a prolonged visit to England each year. One thing seems certain: it was often strained by the unnecessarily complicated way in which Ricketts was paid. He received a percentage of the cost of works the Gallery acquired, but different percentages if he found the work than if he merely gave advice, and again a different amount if the sum for a single work was more than $10,000; and the commission was paid only at the time the purchase was completed. Brown and Ricketts both found this arrangement difficult to interpret, and even the Treasury Board officers were frequently confused.

Another problem arose when Ricketts was not forthright enough in his criticism of a work the Gallery was considering, and which he believed faint praise would damn. When in 1926 the Gallery bought at Jungman in London its second Turner, *The Shipwreck* (plate 75), and a *Venus in a Landscape*, attributed to Reynolds, Ricketts wrote to Brown:

Concerning the Turner, I view the purchase without rapture and I deeply regret the acquisition of the Reynolds which has passed through too many accidents to claim his authorship, it would not surprise me if it turns out as poor Hoppner when cleaned & I doubt if the vague portrait head is part of the original work, the whole thing disquiets and distresses me & I fear, politeness, dislike for the Jungman ambience, and a wish to leave it, prevented my speaking up, let the burden of the purchase rest with the Trustees.

Fortunately, although Ricketts was only too right about the 'Reynolds', the judgement of the Trustees about the Turner seems from a point later in the century to have been sound.

If Ricketts was occasionally too reticent (he soon realized his error and became less so), Brown was occasionally too diffident about his own judgement. When Ricketts recommended the purchase of a *Magdalen* attributed to Van Dyck (it has never been exactly assigned since to any artist or school), Brown wrote:

With regard to the Van Dyck, it looks very interesting and is as you say finely painted I am sure. It is possible that if we can't purchase it that I could interest someone here in it. I find the type of Magdalen rather difficult to enjoy and the action rather sentimental and trivial. It lacks the grand Veronese manner and decoration and not very much to offer in return, so to speak. But the price is marvelous and I am sure the work is probably more convincing than the photograph suggests, so I shall be glad to see it.

Out of respect for Ricketts' enthusiasm Brown found a donor, but he should have heeded his own misgivings.

Clearly Brown and Ricketts needed a third person to listen to their doubts and bring these into the deliberations of the Trustees. The Chairman for most of this time, Dr F. J. Shepherd, does not seem to have been such a man. Indeed, as his biographer, William Boyman Howell, observes: 'One of Shepherd's peculiarities was an inability to bring himself to admit that anyone else knew much about subjects in which he was interested.' Dr Shepherd, a former surgeon who had been an important figure in the development of medicine in Montreal, brought to the Gallery the supreme self-assurance of a Montrealer who collected art (the greatest of these, Sir William Van Horne, whom Shepherd knew, had died in 1915) and who supported the Art Association of Montreal (he was its president from 1906 to 1911 and from 1918 until his death). But he was not a man to clarify the relationship of Ricketts and Brown.

Ricketts' chief contribution to Ottawa's collection appears to have been the acquisition of portraits. (At one point in their correspondence Brown remonstrated with Ricketts about the danger of the National Gallery's becoming a Portrait Gallery.) Significant examples of his guidance here can be seen in the Eworth *Lady Dacre* (plate IX), which was bought with very little apparent excitement, although Brown did know about the recent identification of the artist and about the history of Lady Dacre's unfortunate husband, shown in the picture; Moroni's *Portrait of a Man*, of which Brown wrote to Ricketts after the Trustees had approved its acquisition: 'The portrait is truly magnificent and there can be few better'; and Bronzino's *Portrait of a Man* (plate VIII), about which Ricketts may have exaggerated in having recommended it to Brown as 'one of the two finest Bronzino portraits in the world', though he was certainly right in observing that 'The acquisition of this would add enormously to the superb series of Renaissance portraits.' There was also an interesting addition in a male portrait from Renaissance Germany, then attributed to Bartel Beham.

Perhaps even more important to Ricketts himself were the four Venetian portraits he recommended to the Gallery: the painting that was acquired in 1925 as Sebastiano de Piombo but is now considered to be Bernardino Licinio; the Tintoretto *Servant* in 1927 (plate 16); and the Titian (plate 15) and the fine Cariani (plate 14) in 1928. In a letter of 15 August 1926 Ricketts wrote:

In urging the superb portrait – sometimes described as Tintoretto's Servant – as a purchase for Canada I should like you to tell the Trustees that . . . should it be felt that its purchase would tend to the over-representation of Tintoretto in your gallery – since you already own two fine specimens – I would point out that this would, on the contrary, give character to your collection, of which it could be said that no where else in America was he so well represented.

Two years later he wrote with equal persuasiveness about the Titian and Cariani: 'I now come to the Titian; this I consider a representative and noble work by one of the great masters of all time. Its acquisition would add dignity and weight to the exceptionally good set of Venetian pictures at Ottawa', and of the Cariani, 'this rich and romantic picture is superb in colour and racy in workmanship. It shows the influence of Giorgione.'

Ricketts' enthusiasm for Venetian art and even for Venice itself found a response in Brown and indeed in Shepherd who had discovered Titian, Tintoretto, and Veronese when he visited Venice in 1875. Even today more than half the Venetian pictures in the collection were acquired from the collaboration of Ricketts and Shepherd and Brown. And one of their great bargains, Castiglione's *Worship of Pan*, bought at auction at Christies for £50, though Genoese of the seventeenth century, has a Venetian flavour.

Although both Ricketts and Brown were conscious of the condition of works of art and interested in conservation, they bought Venetian pictures that on the whole have lost the bloom of their original oil glazes. Their most disappointing acquisition may have been the *Adam and Eve* given to Tintoretto. On 15 January 1926 Brown cabled Ricketts: SENT FOR CONSIDERATION TINTORETTO ADAM AND EVE SARGENTS COLLECTION SEE DR MAYER JANUARY APOLLO EXCELLENT CONDITION TWENTY-FIVE HUNDRED POUNDS WHAT DO YOU THINK? BROWN. Ricketts answered: ADVISE PURCHASE THOUGH FINER VERSION EXISTS WRITING. Brown also wrote to Colley, the restorer the Gallery used: 'I believe the Tintoretto can be very much improved and a good deal of dark varnish and some dirt removed. The sky shows traces of blue and I believe this would re-appear. The picture is in marvelous condition, without a trace of restoration and has not even been backed.' After it had been acquired for £2,200 and either Colley had seen it or Brown had looked at it more carefully, Brown wrote to Ricketts: 'Although the Tintoretto has been roughly cleaned, Colley can improve it vastly still, I am sure.' In fact, however, the work has been so abraded, or the colours were so fugitive, that we seem to see more bolus ground and canvas than paint.

It is probably worthwhile at this point to give an aside to F. W. Colley, the restorer in whom Brown at least for some time in the twenties had so much confidence. Although Colley's writing paper had a San Francisco address, he seemed to be constantly on the move, spending his winters in Bermuda and as an itinerant restorer visiting places like Ottawa to clean a number of pictures in an incredibly short time. He had been recommended by a member of the Group of Seven, Arthur Lismer, in a letter of June 1922, as 'a friend of mine, and a most experienced restorer of fine pictures'. In September of that year Brown was writing Walker of this man 'with credentials from New Zealand, Australia, New York, San Francisco and other places', and whom he had tested by having him work on O'Brien's diploma work (plate XXII). On the whole Brown favoured him, adding: 'It is so difficult to find a good man in such a trade and one who never varnishes or repaints is rarer still.' Brown was apparently less enthusiastic about Colley later, but there is no reason to believe that, in terms of his times, he did not do a competent (if maddeningly undocumented) job.

Ricketts gave a final fillip to the Venetian collection by adding four Canalettos in 1929 and 1930. The first, the *Vegetable Market*, seems to have been acquired without much discussion, but Ricketts wanted the other three to be bought, along with the Bronzino portrait and a Neri di Bicci altar (plate 2), to celebrate the fiftieth anniversary of the Gallery, and he even composed a letter to the Prime Minister, Mackenzie King, recommending special appropriations for the works. Ricketts felt he had an entrée with the Prime Minister. He had dined at his house in November 1927, an occasion he described amusingly in a letter to Shannon:

Though I arrived early at the house, met a desiccated he-secretary, and had to wait, I found on contact that I possessed the calm of despair or of renunciation. I was prepared to let things slide – and I think I never have shown greater self-possession, greater felicity of phrase, or a sweeter touch. I was able to hear my own voice. In the course of the dinner the lights were reduced to candles only; this I liked, till I found a sort of hypnotic effect in his attentive face. I had to fence in the matter of the moderns, praise old and new purchases, allow for luck, since the purchase of good pictures is difficult, explain the difficulties of expert knowledge by comparing it to legal acumen, where the evidence is equal, comparing it to the intuitive and exact knowledge of a doctor, who sometimes knows without looking, at other times having to test and grope endlessly. I had allowed him to talk about his farm, his wish to rebuild the town. I put in my stunts about Mussolini, my parable of the Sibyl and the Sibylline Books to account for the soaring of picture prices. I spoke charmingly about his late mother in front of an awful picture, and got him voluble on the question of the Carillon in the town – I thought he wanted to kiss me when I said a child born in Ottawa might remember it all his life.

From New York he wrote to Cecil Lewis: 'I had to remain on to persuade the Premier to make an emergency grant of £10,000, the day after he had agreed to grant the site for the National Gallery costing thousands. Imagine Baldwin being approached, and agreeing. . . . I told the Trustees, who were frightened that the thing was impossible, that I would only eat and drink and be polite. Then the spirit moved me and I deliberately set about to fascinate the man. I could hear my own voice, and strangely enough I usually don't. *I did the trick.*'

It is not certain that he did the trick again in 1930, but the works he wanted were acquired. In recommending the three Canalettos he was astute enough to note that two 'are of an unusual type and in a richer scale of colouring than is usual with Canaletto'. These views of the Arsenale (plate 39) and the Piazzetta are now given to Canaletto's nephew Bellotto, and were presumably painted before he left Venice for Dresden and Warsaw.

Ricketts was also proud of two acquisitions made in 1927. One was

Luini's *The Christ Child and St John with a Lamb* (plate 13), of which he wrote: 'Concerning the Luini I consider it a most typical example of his Art when under the influence of Leonardo da Vinci and it reveals this fascinating Italian painter in the most winning and engaging aspect of his art.' He was even more enthusiastic – and more enthusiastic than scholars are today – about the Botticelli *Two Children* (plate 5), which he included in the 1930 Burlington House exhibition of Italian art. He wrote to Brown: 'I would like you to congratulate the Trustees on my behalf for their courage and foresightedness in buying the Botticelli. I am aware that, to many not acquainted with the prices now given for early Italian paintings [owing to their approaching total disappearance from the market], the cost may seem high [it was £6,000]. . . . I would be so pleased if you would read this letter to the Trustees, it is rare that an expert wishes to say nice things to his overlords.'

During this period Eric Brown, who in 1924 was elected President of the (American) Association of Art Museum Directors, had his own adventures. Some of these were thanks to his friendship with the Government Anthropologist, Marius Barbeau, who also had offices in the Victoria Museum. Barbeau persuaded Brown to make the Gallery's first purchase of the wood carvings of Québec. During their preparations for a joint exhibition on the Canadian Indian, Barbeau suggested that Brown should see Emily Carr, a British Columbian painter of Indian subjects. In her autobiography, *Growing Pains*, Miss Carr describes the visit from the Browns in 1927. At that time, in desperation, she had given up painting and was running a boarding house in Victoria, B.C. 'To be reminded that I had once been an Artist hurt,' she wrote of the telephone call she received from Brown, of whom she had never heard, representing the National Gallery of which she also had never heard. Brown arrived in Victoria and persuaded Miss Carr to lend fifty canvases to the exhibition and offered her a railway pass to come east to see it; he also bought three works for the collection (including plate 124). Emily Carr did come east and wrote: 'The Ottawa show was a success. All the familiar things of my West – totem poles, canoes, baskets, pictures (a large percentage of the pictures were mine). It embarrassed me to see so much of myself exhibited. The only big show I had been in before was the Salon d'Automne in Paris.' This trip put her in touch for the first time with artists of eastern Canada; it was particularly important for her because she discovered Lawren Harris of the Group of Seven and his work. Harris wrote to her of the exhibition: 'I feel you have found a way of your own wonderfully suited to the Indian spirit, Indian feeling for life and nature. The pictures are works of art in their own right . . . have creative life in them . . . they breathe.'

In this period one work for the European collection was found in Canada. Brown wrote about it in an article called 'Adventures in Museum Buying' in *The Arts* of February 1926:

It is so exceedingly rare that any of the pictures brought into an art gallery by the casual owner ever turns out to possess the least possible value, as I am sure any director will testify, that a really interesting picture acquired in this way is something of an event and improves one's faith in mankind. A small, obviously seventeenth-century Italian picture, a 'Baptism of Christ', was a recent example of this. It had certainly been through a fire, it was flapping loose from its stretcher and stained with the neglect of the ages, but its few undisclosed parts gave promise of something more interesting than usual, and the promise was more than fulfilled for . . . it turned out to be sound enough craftsmanship of the good old artistic days.

This was actually a Dutch painting (plate 21), signed by Bloemaert; it was happily in sound condition. For it the Gallery paid its owner, the Hon. Mr Justice Lucien Dubuc of Edmonton, one hundred dollars, so it should properly be regarded as his gift.

In a letter to a friend in the winter of 1930–1, Ricketts summed up what he had accomplished with Brown and the Trustees and an average of $80,000 a year to spend on works of art: 'In the last six years we have laid the foundations of an exceptionally fine provincial Gallery containing fine specimens of some of the great names in art.'

5 1930–1939
Brown and Southam

On Dr Shepherd's death in 1929 H. S. Southam became the third Chairman of the Board and the first Ottawa member; he was therefore Chairman during the last two years of Ricketts' association with the Gallery. Southam would have satisfied the 1907 Privy Council's requirements that a Trustee should be a gentleman who had shown an interest in and appreciation of art, for he had a fine collection of nineteenth-century painting and was even to venture into the twentieth century with the purchase of an early Cubist Picasso that is now in the collection of the Museum of Modern Art, New York. In addition, as a member of a family that owned one of Canada's largest newspaper groups, and as publisher of the influential *Ottawa Citizen*, his requests for assistance for the National Gallery could not easily be ignored. In fact the year Southam became Chairman, Brown was able to write to Arthur Lismer, a member of the Group of Seven: 'We are gaining ground in public estimation here enormously. H. S. Southam, as Chairman of the Board, has already had a marvellous effect on our other friend [Mackenzie King] and all sorts of developments are loosening up.'

Southam was also ready to give the Gallery financial assistance when it could not otherwise acquire a work for its collection. He had persuaded his father to present the *Magdalen* attributed to Van Dyck when it was recommended by Ricketts in 1930. A happier purchase that same year was his own: the *Portrait of a Canon* (plate 6), about which Ricketts had written to Brown on 27 September 1929: 'I consider it superb and in fine condition. It is just under life size, the hands and linen are admirable. . . . I prefer not to ascribe it, my personal belief is that it is probably just over the Flemish border in Holland (but I feel out of my depth). It is a most impressive and showy work which I think *the public would like*.' Brown wrote him: 'Whoever painted it was a master and I do not know when I have seen anything more delightful and interesting. I do hope the finances can be arranged so that we can get it.

Mr Southam is greatly taken with it and I have great hopes that once it gets here it will not return.' Southam, who could appreciate a good painting without an artist's name attached to it, made certain it remained in Ottawa.

As a native of Ottawa Southam may have felt a particular personal responsibility for the development of the Gallery's collection. On 12 December 1933 he informed the Board that in his will he was leaving twenty-three paintings from his collection to the National Gallery and that these were valued at $214,000. He explained he was announcing this bequest in order to be able to use it as a lever to encourage others to give to the National Gallery. Three of the twenty-three he intended for the Gallery were undoubtedly given during his lifetime: one Courbet in 1947 and two others in 1950. (The Daumier he gave in 1950 was a later purchase.) Political and financial considerations were to make him change his mind about his bequest, but in the thirties his intentions were genuine and the prospect of the gift must have influenced the Gallery's buying. To an exhibition of 'French Painting of the Nineteenth Century' at the Gallery in January 1934 Southam lent three Courbets, a Boudin, two Corots, a Gauguin, two Van Goghs, an Ingres, a Jongkind, a Pissarro, and a Sisley. Presumably these indicated the nature of his intended bequest.

It was probably on the basis of the knowledge of the Southam collection and that of another Ottawa collector, Gordon C. Edwards, from whom the Gallery in 1946 would buy a Cézanne, a Daumier, a Monet, and two Pissarros, that W.G. Constable, then the Assistant Director of the National Gallery, London, when asked by the Trustees to make a report on Canada's National Gallery in 1931, advised: 'the prices of much modern work, especially that of the French School of the second half of the nineteenth century, are considerably inflated. . . . Moreover, the great number of pictures still in private hands increases the likelihood of the Gallery obtaining them by gift or bequest.'

Out of his interest in stimulating gifts and bequests Southam was able to persuade a newspaper colleague, J.W. McConnell of Montreal, to pay for a painting already acquired for the National Gallery. He was given the choice of either the *Crucifixion of St Andrew* (plate 20), attributed to Ribera (now given to Luca Giordano), for £600, or the Van Dyck *Christ Blessing the Children* (plate 22) for £3,000. McConnell chose the Ribera. In 1931 Southam had been less successful in trying to convince a famous industrialist that he should give a Loutherbourg (plate 75). The reply was: 'I am not feeling so philanthropic this morning, Harry, that I would want to buy this picture and donate it to the gallery. It may be a beautiful piece and historically important. Some time when I am feeling particularly generous, I might possibly, though this is not a promise, be induced to do something with a picture by a Canadian Artist, but just now, please count me out.' Southam was also turned down by a Senator, who wrote: 'At the same time, I think you are doing something that no Chairman has ever done before; namely, attempting to interest the public in our National Gallery, and I wish you every success . . . . If one of these days we feel inclined to make a presentation to the Gallery, as I hope to do, it would be in the way of modern paintings. I have always felt that our Gallery has specialized too much in the old masters, considering the small funds at their disposal and I always marvel how they have been able to do as well as they have.' These prejudices in favour of Canadian and modern art have remained constant factors in private Canadian support of the arts.

The one great hope for the National Gallery was the acquisition of the collection formed by Sir William Van Horne who had died in 1915. In his 1931 report to the Trustees W. G. Constable emphasized

the vital importance to Canada of securing for the National Gallery the collection of works of art formed by the late Sir William C. Van Horne, at present in Montreal. It contains at least sixty pictures of very high merit, which would strengthen the Gallery at its weakest points, and combined with the present collection, put Canada in possession of one of the half dozen finest collections on the American continent. Of special importance in this respect are the groups of paintings by Rembrandt, Hals, Velázquez, El Greco, Zurbarán and Goya and the Dutch landscape painters.

He suggested means of acquiring it, including 'purchase either by the Government as an exceptional measure, or by the Trustees'. These expectations of tapping private resources in Canada must be considered as part of the background against which purchases were made in the thirties.

For Eric Brown, H. S. Southam should have been the perfect Chairman of the Board. He lived in Ottawa and was therefore on hand to give advice; as an Ottawa resident he was more inclined to be generous to the Gallery. In addition he was, like Eric Brown and the Assistant Director of the National Gallery, H. O. McCurry, a convert to Christian Science. This may explain Brown's optimism and equanimity in spite of the Depression. It may also have been responsible for the number of religious works – none of them physically harrowing – that the Trustees, unlike most trustees of North American museums, were prepared to acquire: *Job,* a *Virgin and Child,* a *Rest on the Flight into Egypt,* a *Head of Christ, Christ Blessing the Children,* a *Betrayal of Christ.*

Brown's relationship with the Trustees was not, however, always ideal. On 2 January 1929 he wrote crankily to Ricketts, who was becoming a thorn in his flesh:

It is natural that you should not realize my difficulties but that, unfortunately, does not lessen them. . . . I have one Trustee particularly who never ceases his efforts to reduce my position to nothing and would, if he got to know about such a thing as your demand in the Titian matter, do anything and everything to destroy our agreement together. . . . One Trustee would prefer to see the National Gallery in Mr Carter's hands [we are not quite certain who Mr Carter was], *another would like to see it in his own for the benefit of his friends and, with only five Trustees, the margin is not great.*

Two years later he was writing to Constable: 'Massey is off to China and is out of the picture and Southam is so retiring, owing to being a political opponent of the present government, that it leaves me practically alone to get things moving.'

Something of the nature of the relationship of Brown to the Trustees at this period may be found in his correspondence with Southam about the acquisition in 1938 of the Rigaud (plate XV): 'I see a very fine example of the work of Honoré [actually Hyacinthe] Rigaud, signed and dated 1699, coming up for sale at Sotheby's on February 23rd . . . and I would recommend it to the Trustees that we commission Colnaghi to buy it for us up to £900 at a 10% commission'; he went on to explain that Byam Shaw of Colnaghi's had cabled him that its owner had bought it at a country sale for £500 in 1930. The same day (12 February 1938), Southam replied:

I hardly know what to say in reply to your proposal regarding the large painting by H. Rigaud. . . . I have a feeling I would rather save our money for paintings by more important artists, or what I think are more important artists, in view of the fact that the wall space of the National Gallery is so limited and will perhaps continue to be so for some years to come. However, as you recommend the purchase of this painting, I am willing to approve this recommendation, although I do not see why we should offer to pay £900 for this painting when it was bought for £500 at the tail-end of an inflationary period.

Notwithstanding the foregoing views mildly questioning the wisdom or desirability of this purchase, I realize that recommendations for purchase are the responsibility of the Director, and you can put me down as approving this one in response to your request.

Brown thereupon wired Vincent Massey, another member of the Board who was in London, who cabled: HAVE INSPECTED RIGAUD AND LIKE IT STOP DIRECTOR OF LOUVRE WHO HAPPENS TO BE IN LONDON SPEAKS WELL OF IT STOP AM INSTRUCTING COLNAGHI TO SECURE PICTURE AT MAXIMUM SIX HUNDRED ON BASIS OF YOUR TELEGRAM. Brown was worried that he should have reduced the maximum from £900 to £600, but on 23 February 1938 Massey cabled: HAVE PURCHASED RIGAUD FOR TWO HUNDRED AND SIXTY POUNDS.

The financial instincts of both Southam and Massey were undoubtedly correct. Nevertheless, in writing to Brown that 'recommendations for purchase are the responsibility of the Director', Southam established an important principle. It is clear that Brown had more independence and authority now than he had even in the ideal relationship with Sir Edmund Walker or in the period in which, largely with Dr Shepherd as Chairman, Ricketts was adviser to the Gallery.

One Trustee who, as we have just seen, could be most helpful was Vincent Massey. 'I was made a Trustee of the National Gallery in Ottawa in 1925,' he wrote in his memoirs *What's Past is Prologue*, 'and served until I went to Government House in 1952 – for the last four years, as chairman. The money provided by the government was not lavish, and the temporary quarters provided by the Gallery until quite recently most inadequate. But careful buying made possible a collection modest in size but excellent in quality.'

In the background of these years was the Depression and the imminence of a Second World War. As Brown wrote to Constable on 3 September 1931: 'All governments are sweating to tide over a difficult winter and art does not bulk large in their horizon.' In the eight years between the death of Ricketts and the death of Brown, only about half the amount of money that had been spent as an average when Ricketts had been adviser was available for the acquisition of works of art. In Ricketts' time it had averaged about $80,000 a year, in the thirties $40,000. But the problem was that appropriations were by no means regular; in 1928–9 the Gallery had $113,910.59 for acquisitions, in 1934–5 the amount dropped to $5,217.68.

In spite of these gloomy statistics it was a period of golden opportunity because the market for works of art was deflated and there was little competition. We have already seen that a large and important Luca Giordano could be bought for £600, a major early Van Dyck for £3,000, and a splendid Rigaud at auction for £260 (with agent's fees it cost the Gallery £291/2/3). In addition, possibly the finest Loutherbourg in existence (plate 72) was bought from Knoedler in London for £800 and the *Job* by Lievens (plate 25) was generously acquired for the National Gallery of Canada by the National Arts Collection Fund in Great Britain for £400 at auction at Sotheby's.

Murillo's *Two Monks*, admittedly damaged by fire, cost £850 and the large Stomer (plate 26) £120. Even the El Greco *St Francis* (plate 36) and the *Rest on the Flight into Egypt* by Veronese (plate 17) were bought together at Agnew's for only $41,366.66. One of the Gallery's most important acquisitions, the Piero di Cosimo (plate V), was bought from Schaeffer in New York for $25,000. The Jusepe Leonardo (plate 37) cost £700, a large Kneller £1,250, the Le Brun (plate 34) £350, the Claude (plate 33) £1,500. Historically important Canadian works were acquired for next to nothing: the *Self-Portrait* by the eighteenth-century painter, François Beaucourt (plate 101), for $100 and Plamondon's *Sister Saint-Alphonse* (plate XX) for $500 in 1937.

Brown was acting on his own. Although in her biography of her husband Maud Brown thought of W. G. Constable as a successor to Ricketts as her husband's adviser, he was actually employed only to write a report on the Gallery's activities in 1931 and to make a lecture tour across the country in 1933. But he was a sympathetic correspondent, ready to pass on tips and give generous and valuable advice without trying to force decisions upon his friend. He himself has described Brown in London:

He had an excellent nose for a good picture while his friendliness and integrity won him respect and liking in the art market, so that, during a few weeks' stay in England, he would see most of what the market had to show, not only among the big dealers but among the smaller men in the world of the runner and marchand amateur. *At this point his museum friends would be brought into consultation, mainly concerning problems of authenticity, condition and price; and so armed he would make the final decision.*

In this period his nose led him to baroque art.

Although Constable had in his report praised the Gallery for making acquisitions on the basis of aesthetic rather than historic considerations and had written, 'In present circumstances a policy of gap-filling is to be deprecated; quality, not type should be the criterion', Brown's approach was more historical than Walker's had been. In a 1933 broadcast over the Canadian Radio Commission he stated: 'The policy of the National Gallery has always been to build up both the finest possible collection of European art of the greatest periods and the most complete and representative collection of Canadian art in existence.' The acquisitions of the early Murillo, the Stomer, the El Greco, the Van Dyck, the Luca Giordano, the Jusepe Leonardo, the Kneller, the Le Brun, the Rigaud, a painting attributed to Rembrandt, and the Claude (which Constable had first brought out for consideration in

Boston) suggest that Brown felt the 'greatest period' neglected in the Gallery's collection was the baroque. (We have no statement from him to corroborate this, though there is perhaps confirmation in the purchase of a film called *Baroque Art* in 1936.) Brown was also conscious of history in recommending the acquisition of French art. Writing to Southam about the Rigaud, for example, he said: 'This period of French painting is particularly interesting to Canada and Canadians.'

This does not mean that Brown had no eye for quality; his choices seemed surer and his judgement about condition more confident than in the past. He went beyond the seventeenth century, as when he welcomed Constable's suggestion that the Gallery consider the Loutherbourg *A Midsummer Afternoon with a Methodist Preacher*, available at Knoedler in London and a work that still enlivens the eighteenth-century English collection. And certainly both his eye and sense of historic appropriateness were satisfied with the acquisition of the great fifteenth-century *Vulcan and Aeolus* (plate V) by Piero di Cosimo from a New York dealer. In this period of his greatest independence most of his acquisitions were made in London, many from Tomas Harris.

Brown was concerned that the collection of drawings was not keeping up with the collection of prints that Rossiter's successor as Curator of Prints and Drawings, Miss Kathleen Fenwick, had maintained in spite of the Depression. She had managed to continue to buy some remarkable impressions, on rare occasions with Rossiter's advice, always based on her own remarkable eye for quality. At her suggestion Brown wrote to Constable in 1931 to ask about appointing someone in London, in particular Paul Oppé, to buy drawings for the Gallery. Constable recommended Oppé highly: 'A point that should be mentioned is that Oppé is on friendly terms with most of the collectors in this country and knows most of the museum people; and being a man who is not afraid to ask other people what they think, he would be able to bring the learning of others to reinforce gaps in his own.' It was six years, however, before Oppé was appointed. For the last two years of his life Brown was once more engaged with Oppé in one of those correspondences, which he so much enjoyed, about the acquisition of works of art. And Oppé, with only $3,000 a year, at a time when the market for drawings was growing, was nevertheless able to make some amazingly good buys. The most remarkable purchase before Brown's death may have been the *Old Oak Tree, Shoreham, Kent* (plate 182) by Samuel Palmer for £50, the chalk *Presentation of the Virgin* (plate 159) by Jacopo Bassano for £65, and a small metalpoint attributed to Raphael for £165 (plate 157).

Eric Brown always had a strong sense of responsibility for the physical care of the works of art in the collection, which the members of the Advisory Council and the Board of the National Gallery shared. As Director, Brown had a powerful ally in a remarkable man, George Harbour, who had been apprenticed as a framer and gilder in England before coming to Canada in 1887. He worked in Ottawa for Jas. Wilson and Sons, which from the beginning of the Gallery's history had done most of its framing and even sold it an occasional picture. When Harbour came to work for the Gallery in 1912 he played two roles – both important for the protection of works of art. He was the superintendent in charge of packing and hanging and the nearest thing to a conservator the Gallery possessed. 'The fundamentals of true craftsmanship were inbred in him', Maud Brown has written, 'and his sense of justice and order commanded respect. . . . George received his training in the excellent system of apprenticeship that has hardly changed since the Middle Ages. As a skilled artisan, he knew his tools and materials to perfection. . . . Through the years George gained a sound knowledge of picture restoration.' A notebook in the Gallery records his care of frames (and more cursorily of pictures) from November 1912 to May 1922. He would write, for example, of the frame of West's *Death of Wolfe* in April 1921 that it was 'gilt in oil with gold leaf . . . toned in size colour and finished with a spirit lacquer. Fourteen (14) books of gold were used, and at prevailing rates when the frame was made in 1912, the frame was worth $325.' Of the picture itself he only added: 'At the same time the painting was washed, re-layed and burnished with Mastic varnish.' Although the more important European works were at one time given to an itinerant restorer like F. W. Colley, and eventually sent to the conservator working at the Museum of Fine Arts in Boston, Harbour became increasingly adept at the more routine restoration jobs, which he handled conservatively and competently. By 1935 Eric Brown was arguing that the Gallery should set up its own conservation studio under Harbour: 'During the past 12 years he has specialized in the study of picture restoration, studying not only at the National Gallery but at the Boston Museum of Fine Arts and elsewhere. There is no doubt that by his initiative he has acquired an amount of expert knowledge and technical skill.'

In 1938, before his approaching retirement (he was by then sixty-seven), Harbour was given his first apprentice to train. He insisted that this young man, who had his B.Sc. in chemistry, spend six months learning about packing, framing, and handling pictures before he touched a work of art. The Gallery's Senior Conservator, Mervyn Ruggles, can now forget his youthful irritation with these tasks in his gratitude for the lessons of patience, caution, and an inherent respect for the sanctity of the work of art, as the artist had conceived it, which George Harbour transmitted to him.

During this period Brown became troubled about the Gallery's and his own relationship to contemporary Canadian art. In this area he met constant opposition because of his support of Tom Thomson and the Group of Seven. This had been a matter of discussion in the House, the subject of letters to the editor and long editorials across the country, and the reason for continuing animosity on the part of the Royal Canadian Academy. While Walker was alive, Brown had a Chairman who bore the brunt of all the criticisms himself. On Walker's death Brown was in the forefront of the action, and he handled opposition adroitly throughout preparations for the two Wembley exhibitions. When it broke out again in 1931, however, he lost heart.

Encouraged by a change of government that year, 118 artists headed by Wyly Grier, who had been best man at the Browns' wedding, sent the new Prime Minister, R. B. Bennett, and the Governor-General the following protest:

The petition of the undersigned members of the Royal Canadian Academy, Ontario Society of Artists, Graphic Arts Society, British Columbia Art Society, Palette & Chisel Club, Vancouver Sketch Club, and the Islands Arts & Crafts Society of Victoria humbly ask your consideration of the following protests.

1   The National Gallery has for years exhibited a flagrant partisanship in selecting and hanging pictures at the Annual Exhibition held in Ottawa.
2   That the Directors of the National Gallery have selected and distributed works at home and abroad that do not represent the best in Canadian Art.
3   That the continuance of the policy will inevitably lead to misunderstandings and to the possibility of our best artists withholding their work from the National Gallery.
4   This document is the true and expressed opinion by artists from coast to coast given independently of their affiliations with organized societies or groups.

H. G. Jones and Edmond Dyonnet in their history of the Royal Canadian Academy explained the matter further:

The Progressives, as we have called them, may be represented as being delighted over National Gallery support of their cause, for year after year it had continued by exhibition, propaganda and purchase to be quite notoriously their most ardent and substantial supporter . . . the most numerous group was roused to resentment by the spectacle of a government agency using its power, influence and money to maintain a controversial position in current art movements; a sort of Mussolini of Canadian art – acted by the director – was seen in the background.

This was not an official Academy protest, but since Grier, its president, was in the vanguard, it was difficult to make the distinction. A. Y. Jackson felt it provided sufficient reason to resign from the Academy.

Among the artists who signed the petition were Franz Johnston (five of whose works the Gallery owned), an original member of the Group of Seven; George Reid, who had been instrumental in arousing the government's interest in the Gallery in 1907; Horatio Walker, from whom the Gallery had bought a painting for $10,000 in 1911; and the Ottawa painter Franklin Brownell, from whom the Gallery had bought thirteen paintings and for whom it had held a retrospective exhibition in 1922.

Brown, whose relationship with women artists had always been remarkably good – perhaps because, with such an intelligent and attractive wife as Maud Brown, he appreciated their strengths and virtues – found them organizing his defence. Two of his supporters were the Toronto sculptors Frances Loring and Florence Wyle, who shared a house and studio and were always known affectionately as 'The Girls'. Although there were bronzes by both of them in the Canadian War Memorials Collection, the Gallery had bought only one small work by Loring, the *Derelicts*, in 1929 and nothing from Wyle since 1918. The secretary for the defence was another sculptor, Elizabeth Wyn Wood; happily the Gallery *had* bought works in recent years by her and her husband Emanuel Hahn (plate 138). With the Girls behind her, Wyn Wood managed to collect over 300 artists' signatures to a petition stating: 'We, the undersigned artists, believe the policy of the National Gallery of Canada to be fair to all Canadian artists and all phases of Canadian art, and we have full confidence in the Trustees and the Director, Mr Eric Brown, and in their administration of the Gallery.' Some of the artists who signed were sufficiently selfless to forget that the Gallery had not bought their works. This was true of both Miller Brittain of Saint John, N. B., who died two years before the Gallery bought one of his paintings in 1970, and Bertram Brooker of Toronto, who died fourteen years before the Gallery acquired its first works by this artist in 1969 (plate 137). The first purchase of a work by Jean-Paul Lemieux of Québec (plate 147) was not made until 1956, by Jack Bush of Toronto (plate 151) until 1966, and by Ernest Lindner of Saskatoon until 1968. And yet they signed.

David Milne, an artist from whom the Gallery had bought only six drawings, although his works were represented in the War Memorials Collection, released a barrage of letters to editors in January and February 1933. On 6 January he wrote of the protest to a Toronto paper:

It is, in effect, an attempt by the leaders of the R. C. A. to bring pressure to bear on the National Gallery and dominate its selection of works of art for exhibition or purchase by the nation. If the R.C.A. represented Canadian art as a whole and were responsible to the people of Canada the movement would make some appeal to reason. However, though it's under royal patronage and received a considerable grant from the Dominion Government, the academy is neither representative nor responsible.

He went on to enlarge on other academies, saying that 'The group of seven is an interesting example of an academy in formation', and concluding: 'it is time to point out that the only institution that can claim to represent the art of all Canada and the only one over which the people of Canada have any control, is the National Gallery.' In another letter on 26 January to the Ottawa *Journal* he said: 'Twenty-five years ago it was little more than a lumber room, a repository for diploma pictures, copies and odds and ends of art.' On 7 January he had written to Elizabeth Wyn Wood:

I have already taken the liberty of sending a letter to the Prime Minister and another to the Chairman of the Board of Trustees expressing satisfaction with the work of the National Gallery so far as I know it. Frankly the only way to frustrate the aims of the petitioners is to make more noise than they do (perhaps more intelligible noise, but still noise) . . . . If there is any chance of this matter reaching the floor of the house (probably there isn't) it would seem advisable to supply all members with an expression of confidence in the N.G. and a statement of facts – not so much for information as for flattery. One phase of this agitation is unfortunate even though no action is taken by the government, there will still be pressure on the National Gallery, enough to interfere with its freedom.

It is good to report that three years later Vincent Massey and his wife gave the Gallery its first three canvases by this defender of the institution, and that, with a gift of 1970 from the Douglas M. Duncan estate, the Gallery now has more works by David Milne than by any other artist.

Brown's reaction to the criticism was natural. On 2 September 1932 he wrote to Constable:

I am getting rather doubtful of the wisdom of trying to push Canadian art forward as much as we do. For the past fifteen years we have purchased, exhibited and circulated it, fed the young museums and art societies and generally propogated it in every possible way, but its growth and development is accompanied by many pains . . . . I am thinking over the possibility of pulling out of it to some extent. . . . We are a sort of National Gallery and a National Gallery of British Art combined and get all the criticism that comes to both. . . . If I can get the Trustees to agree, I think it would be wise to withdraw from current art activities gradually or at least temporarily so as to give us time for more study and some peace of mind at least.

Constable answered him promptly:

It is rather presumptuous of me to speak but from the little I saw in Canada and from a great deal I hear I sincerely hope that you will not retire from the battle prematurely. I know how exasperating and disheartening squabbles about modern painting can be. . . . Personally I do not think the intelligent study of old masters can be divorced from the study of modern work and I hold that each branch of activity stimulates and helps the other.

Brown did not give up. In 1938, the very year before he died, he organized an exhibition called 'A Century of Canadian Art' at the Tate Gallery, London, and spoke about it enthusiastically for the B.B.C. in his only television appearance, which was in fact one of the first telecasts ever to be made on the arts. Ironically, although Milne in his letter to Elizabeth Wyn Wood said 'what a beautiful and final solution' it would be if 'some royal honour' should be conferred 'on the efficient and long-suffering Director of the N.G.', it was instead his opponent Wyly Grier who was knighted in 1935.

Eric Brown had accomplished almost everything on his own without the support of a trained staff later Directors took for granted. He was well described by Constable: 'This tall, slim and elegant figure, wearing a monocle, scarcely seemed to jibe with what I know of Canadian art and artists. But it needed only a few minutes to reveal the simplicity, the shrewdness and the enthusiasm which made him so immediately attractive.' After his death Emily Carr wrote to Mrs Brown: 'I owe him so much, for I was overwhelmed by despair about my work when he came West and pulled me out and made me start again.' Kenneth Clark, the Director of the National Gallery, London, wrote: 'Eric Brown was known to all lovers of arts in the English-speaking world as one of the most sensitive and distinguished of all gallery directors. He understood painting as an artist, but he retained the detachment of the critic. He was, in fact, a supremely civilized mind in which great enthusiasm was concealed by irony, humour and tolerance.' With all of these qualities he established the direction of the National Gallery of Canada as an institution. In the more than twenty years since his death, there has not been one development that Eric Brown did not anticipate.

6   1939–1955
Great Years of Collecting

Eric Brown died suddenly on 6 April 1939. By the end of the month he was replaced by the man who had been his Assistant Director and the Board's Secretary for twenty years, Harry Orr McCurry. His appointment was so logical that every artists' society in Canada pressed it upon the government and the Trustees. McCurry, who had entered government service the same year as Brown, came to the National Gallery in 1919 and, to quote Maud Brown, 'his integrity and business ability became immediately apparent, and his faithful service continued throughout the years'. He had another advantage in that, through his wife and his mother-in-law (both of whom had charmed Ricketts), he was part of the circle of Mackenzie King who, except for the period 1930–5, had been Prime Minister of Canada since 1921.

McCurry's first six years as Director of the National Gallery embraced another difficult period in its history: the Second World War. Although in his annual reports he might try to point out that the continued large attendances proved there was a genuine public need for the Gallery's activities in wartime, and that even in Great Britain appropriations for art had been reduced only four per cent, his budget was as low as $43,720 in 1941–2 and 1942–3, with nothing whatsoever for acquisitions. He valiantly tried to compensate for this by emphasizing the educational program, by launching a series of films on Canadian artists with the National Film Board, by collaborating on broadcasts on art to schools, for which the Gallery printed and distributed over 120,000 small reproductions in 1944–5, and by publishing in large quantities reproductions for distribution to the armed services and others overseas and throughout Canada.

From 13 December 1939 until 1 October 1946 a quorum could never be obtained for a meeting of the Board, of which Southam was Chairman. McCurry merely signed an annual statement himself. The one relief from the austerity of these times was provided by the Chairman, who gave a great Poussin to the collection in 1944; this was the idyllic *Landscape with a Woman Bathing* (plate 35), which was described in the *Annual Report* as 'a dark, dramatic canvas in the artist's characteristic classical manner'. It had been hanging in the Gallery for some years.

McCurry theoretically had the advice of W. G. Constable, who was by then Curator of Paintings at Boston's Museum of Fine Arts and who had been given permission by his Director to be Ottawa's unpaid consultant as long as 'the work would primarily be advice on questions of authenticity, condition and the general desirability of pictures'. In actuality Constable did not lead McCurry to acquisitions but provided him with reassurance. There is nothing in the Gallery's records to suggest that McCurry used Constable as a sounding board in the way Brown had done.

At the time of Brown's death McCurry had been visiting dealers in New York. One of them wrote on the very day Brown died concerning the portrait of Boyer by Cézanne (plate 50): 'I hope that you will be able to enthuse your colleague [i.e. Brown] and Board of Trustees sufficiently to make them have it sent up to the gallery to be seen.' Almost a year later McCurry asked Constable about it, adding: 'It is, of course, an early picture and not tremendously important but both Mr Southam and I like it.' Its acquisition *was* important as the first Cézanne to enter the collection. In addition McCurry bought *Le Pont de Narni* by Corot (plate 43) about which Constable was also consulted and which represented a milestone as a historically important work (the first Corot exhibited at the Paris Salon) and one of real quality from the first half of the nineteenth century in France.

The Gallery's first act after the war was to buy a group of nineteenth-century French works from a private collector, Gordon C. Edwards of Ottawa. This represented two significant departures. One was the acknowledgement that the Gallery could not depend on the donations of private collectors for its French pictures as Constable had suggested in his 1931 report. Indeed the Van Horne heirs were to put most of their collection up for auction at Parke-Bernet in 1946, and Southam had also been selling his. The reality of the situation was softened somewhat by Southam's giving Courbet's *La femme aux gants*, contributing to the purchase of an early landscape by Gauguin in 1947, and giving still another Courbet and a Daumier in 1950. The Edwards family banded together after the death of their father in 1946 and gave the Gallery the largest of its Courbets, *Les Cascades* (plate 45), but on the whole it had to be conceded that French painting since 1850 would have to be acquired for the Gallery by purchase rather than gift.

The second departure was in acknowledging belatedly that this art did have some value and was not – as Brown, Ricketts, and Constable desired or feared – an inflated fad. Brown, of course, had bought the Impressionists – Degas, Monet, Pissarro, and Sisley – but he could not easily accept Cézanne and the next generation. A. Y. Jackson had written in *Saturday Night* as early as 17 December 1932 to show how short-sighted Canadian collectors were about a period in which 'the genius of France has dominated the whole world of art'. He ended ironically: 'To those who look on modern art as a menace it may be reassuring to know that it has not invaded Canada. There is no country in the world where it has made less impression. Of late years the Cézannes, Van Goghs and Gauguins have gone up so much in value that there is no longer any danger of their coming to Canada.' The Director and Trustees were ready to face that 'danger' fifteen years later and even within twenty years to make a timid response to Jackson's question 'Who owns a Derain? a Picasso? a Matisse? a Léger? or a Braque?' by buying a Fauve Braque (plate 59) and a Derain (plate 58).

Having undertaken this change in policy, McCurry and the Trustees made use of three principal avenues for their acquisition: the Edwards collection in Ottawa; part of the estate of the late Paris dealer Ambroise Vollard, which had been sequestrated at the Gallery during the war; and blocked currency in the Netherlands. The group of five pictures bought from Edwards would not rock conservative Canada, for they contained a mild Monet seascape, two pleasant Pissarros (including plate 47), a gentle Cézanne painted at Auvers, and the famous final version of Daumier's *Third-Class Carriage* (plate XXI). From the Vollard heirs the Gallery bought a late and intense Degas pastel (*Race-Track*), two Cézannes (plates 52 and 53), and a limestone *Standing Nude* by Maillol.

The existence of blocked currency in the Netherlands was used by McCurry, who was an adroit politician, as a justification for the acquisition of works of art. As a result the Gallery bought a good deal from Van Wisselingh in Amsterdam, who had always sold to Canadian private collectors but seldom to the Gallery. In addition to the Fauve Braque and Derain already mentioned, a Renoir (plate 56) was bought in 1949, an early Van Gogh flower piece in 1950, a Fauve Vlaminck in 1951, a Bonnard and a Dufy in 1952, a Degas pastel of dancers, a Sérusier and a Sisley in 1953, and the splendid Van Gogh *Iris* (plate XXIV) in 1955. All these acquisitions had one characteristic in common: any one of them could be considered a picture for a private collection rather than for a museum. Perhaps they were chosen out of a longing for the private pictures that had never been given, or because the Trustees were consciously or unconsciously thinking of what would be most appropriate in their own homes.

Once it had begun to buy such pictures – and having money for acquisitions after long periods of austerity – the Gallery seemed insatiable. The year after having bought the Van Gogh flower piece at Van Wisselingh it bought a second at Agnew's and, though it owned four Cézannes, bought a fifth (plate 51) in New York. It was spending headily but achieving such strength in French art of the nineteenth century that when Anthony Blunt, Director of the Courtauld Institute in London, was asked to report to the Trustees on the collection in 1951 he congratulated them on this part of the collection and suggested that they now go after less expensive Italian paintings of the seventeenth century.

Purchases from other schools began modestly with the acquisition from Colnaghi in London of Whistler's *Lillie in our Alley* (plate 84) in 1946 and the fine Wilson (plate 70) from Agnew in 1948. Perhaps encouraged by the magnificent gift to the Canadian people in 1950 of Hobbema's *Two Water-mills* (plate 31) by Queen Juliana of the Netherlands, acquisitions increased in tempo with the purchase of Turner's *Mercury and Argus* (plate XIX) and Murillo's *Abraham and Three Angels* (plate XIV) from Agnew in 1951. In 1953 the Gallery acquired the large Benozzo Gozzoli altarpiece (plate 3) from Drey in New York, the Cranach *Venus* (plate 8), and the German *Madonna of the Flowering Pea* (plate II) from Van Wisselingh.

Although Blunt had been appointed as an adviser to the Gallery in 1948 and recommended the Murillo in that year ('an extremely fine specimen') and the Turner (with some reservations about its condition), he found himself bewildered by the terms of his employment. He was obviously quite unaware of the Gallery's prejudices when he recommended a Toulouse-Lautrec brothel scene, on sale in London for £1,800. About this painting he wrote to McCurry: 'It is a superlative piece of painting and has that savage vitality, which is perhaps his greatest quality'; he then naively went on to mention those very characteristics of which the Chairman and Director would most disapprove: 'it is far from being an agreeable picture or an elevating one.' He was also puzzled by the obvious and embarrassed secretiveness of McCurry in London during the summer of 1952; later he realized it must have been because he was negotiating in Vaduz for the Liechtenstein pictures. When he discovered that these acquisitions had been made without his being consulted he felt even more dubious about his value as an adviser. There was none of the rapport with McCurry that Ricketts had with Brown.

It was in 1952 that the first mention of purchases from the Prince of

Liechtenstein appeared in the minutes of the Board. In that year the acquisition of three pictures was approved: *The Toilet of Esther* (plate XII) by Rembrandt and two small cassone panels by Filippino Lippi (plates IV and 4) for $276,000. They were bought in 1953 through Schab in New York. The next year another group of five was acquired for $363,000 with Agnew in London as agent: these were the Memling (plate III), the Matsys (plate VI), the Beham (plate VII), the Guardi (plate 40), and the Nicolaes Maes (plate 28). Both groups of purchases came within a single fiscal year in which the Gallery spent $699,474 for works of art and over $1,100,000 for its total operation as against nil for acquisitions and $43,720 as a total budget only a dozen years before.

McCurry may have had the support of Vincent Massey until his resignation in 1952 and of Southam until his death in 1954, and of such astute Trustees as Cleveland Morgan of Montreal and John MacAulay of Winnipeg, but he himself was largely responsible for having engineered these remarkable acquisitions and the support of the government in buying them. Who actually selected the works still seems a matter of doubt; it may have been the Prince of Liechtenstein himself. In announcing the second group, McCurry had referred to the advice of Constable and Sir Philip Hendy (then Director of the National Gallery, London), but there does not seem to be any evidence that they really determined the choice. However the decision was made, McCurry was clever enough to exploit a report on the arts Vincent Massey had written when he was still a member of the Board and indeed its Chairman. The *Report of the Royal Commission on National Development in the Arts, Letters and Sciences* of 1951 assumes that 'It is the intangibles which give a nation not only its essential character but its vitality as well. What may seem unimportant or even irrelevant under the pressure of daily life may well be the thing which endures, which may give a community its power to survive.' McCurry knowingly echoed this view in announcing the purchase of the second group: 'The combined purchases from the Liechtenstein collection constitute an important investment by the Canadian people which will contribute greatly to the cultural life of the nation.'

For the record it should probably be pointed out that at the April 1954 meeting of the Board its members were determined that the Gallery should have still more works from the Liechtenstein collection, including two Chardins (plates XVI and 41) and the Simone Martini (plate I), which it was not to acquire until after McCurry's retirement in 1955. They also hoped for an option on Leonardo's painting *Ginevra di Benci*, which Paul Mellon was to give Washington in 1967.

The collection was growing – more rapidly in the ten years from the end of the Second World War until the retirement of McCurry than in any other decade in its history. One impressive contribution was the gift by the Rt Hon. and Mrs Vincent Massey of eighty-eight works from the Massey Foundation. These were twentieth-century English paintings (plates 82, 83 and 91) that the Masseys had chosen when he had been Canadian High Commissioner in London from 1935 to 1946. In London Massey had kept a fond place in his thoughts for the National Gallery of Canada. From 1941 he had also been a Trustee of the National Gallery, London, and from 1943 until his return to Canada he was its Chairman. Another important gift came during the war: the bequest by Dr James M. MacCallum of 134 works, most of them by Tom Thomson and the Group of Seven (plate 126). With the works by these same artists that were bought so enthusiastically in the early days by Sir Edmund Walker and Eric Brown, often with the encouragement of MacCallum, the Gallery could now give exhaustive treatment to this nationally important group of painters.

In all this activity the collection of prints and drawings and the Canadian collection were not forgotten. Paul Oppé could not buy during the war, but immediately afterwards he found drawings like the Piranesi (plate 166) and the Rubens (plate 163) for Ottawa. At the same time Kathleen Fenwick was acquiring prints, including a superb first issue of the first edition of Piranesi's *Carceri*, for which Southam paid in 1950, and the *Battle of the Naked Men* by Pollaiuolo in 1952. In 1953 she also bought, among other modern drawings, Picasso's *Young Woman Standing* of 1906 (plate 175) for £400. And she was responsible for buying from the estate of the Earl of Derby a historically important group of watercolours by the English topographer Thomas Davies (1737–1813), who first painted in Canada in 1757 (plate 102).

The Curator of Canadian Art, Robert H. Hubbard, was selecting Canadian works. In 1954 he was given complete responsibility for the choice of contemporary art within a given budget. As a result the Gallery acquired works by artists like Alex Colville (plate 148) and Jean-Paul Riopelle (plate 144), today perhaps the most internationally recognized of Canadian painters. Among the most important additions to the historic collection was the gift of William Berczy's *The Woolsey Family* of 1809 (plate XVIII) by an heir.

McCurry, in addition to building a collection, was building a staff. R.H. Hubbard, a Canadian with a Ph.D. in the history of art, became Curator of Canadian Art in 1947 and was to become the Gallery's Chief Curator and the author of its catalogues. Another young Canadian scholar, trained at Harvard and the Courtauld, William S. A. Dale, was appointed an

Assistant Curator, and in an interrupted series of appointments was to be its Assistant Director, Acting Director, and Deputy Director. Mervyn Ruggles, who had been hired by Brown, was Conservator and documented his work more carefully than had ever been done before in the Gallery's history.

The National Gallery of Canada had always felt that there should be a record of its collection in printed form. As a result, catalogues that were essentially check lists with biographies of the artists were published from 1887; there were eleven editions between 1912 and 1948. It is instructive to examine the 1940 catalogue, which must have been prepared in the directorship of Eric Brown. The emphasis was upon rather romanticized biographies, which varied considerably in length and accuracy; individual works were given only a title and dimensions, not even an inscribed date. The first catalogue to follow the form of more scholarly catalogues in institutions like the National Gallery, London, was published under McCurry in 1948. Prepared by Hubbard and Kathleen Fenwick, with Dr Peter Brieger of the Department of Fine Art of the University of Toronto, this was the first effort toward a systematic scholarly investigation of the collection. The biographies were abbreviated, the individual works were described, information was given on dating and attribution, and the history of each work (its provenance, publication, and exhibitions) was documented. Although attributions were seldom changed, suggestions were made that the Honthorst might be by Stomer (plate 26), an Andrea del Sarto school piece by Domenico Puligo, and the Ribera by Luca Giordano.

The ten remarkable years during which McCurry was director after the war will always be remembered chiefly for the growth of the collection (and the budget). An Ottawa critic, Carl Weiselberger, summed up the McCurry period well when he wrote in the *Citizen* on 26 April 1955: 'His office will be linked with the acquisition of the paintings from the famous Liechtenstein Gallery. . . . A few years earlier, with the generous help of the late H. S. Southam, the Gallery's French Collections gained a quality of broadness and depth which is admired abroad. . . . A future writer of the Gallery story might well describe Dr H. O. McCurry's reign as the most important chapter with regard to purchases of paintings.'

7 1955–1960
Euphoria and Martyrdom

On the retirement of McCurry in the summer of 1955 Alan Jarvis became Director of the National Gallery. A Canadian and a practising sculptor, he was the first Director to have studied the history of art formally, having done graduate work at one of the most serious centres for such studies in the world, the Institute of Fine Arts of New York University. He was a tall and handsome man of forty who had a great deal of style. Style was the quality that particularly attracted Vincent Massey, who, like many members of his family, was instinctively an actor; and it was Massey, a Liberal, who recommended Jarvis to the Liberal government of St-Laurent on the advice of Sir Kenneth Clark, the former Director of the National Gallery, London. Jarvis was an enthusiastic propagandist for the arts and for the National Gallery of Canada and he immediately became a popular figure; in his first year as Director he was asked to give over a hundred speeches. He was urbanely informative on television. In addition he was adored by a staff that he both enlarged and indulged. Altogether he was the most attractive Director the National Gallery has ever had.

One of Jarvis's first tasks was to complete the negotiations for what may well have been the last purchase from the Liechtenstein collection. The choice of two Chardins (plates XVI and 41), a Simone Martini (plate I), and a Rubens had already been made, although the Board had wanted a Rubens *Venus* rather than the small *Entombment* after Caravaggio (plate X) it finally acquired. We might regret the *Venus*, but the *Entombment* is also a masterpiece, if on a smaller and quieter scale. All four paintings added to the distinction of the collection.

The acquisition of the Liechtenstein pictures on top of the gifts of the Massey Foundation and the bequest of Dr MacCallum encouraged the Gallery to print new editions of its catalogue which, because of the size of the collection, now had to appear in three volumes – Volume I: *Older Schools* in 1957; Volume II: *Modern European Schools* in 1959: and Volume III: *Canadian School* in 1960. In his forward to the first volume Jarvis modestly pointed out that 'It is due to my predecessors that the consideration of quality always came first, and that the collection enjoys its present reputation.' He himself was responsible for two important aspects of the publication. One was that, at his encouragement, Hubbard, the author of the catalogues, added further scholarly information and accepted the changes in attribution that had only been suggested in the 1948 edition. The other was a deep concern for their appearance as prestige publications of the Gallery and the University of Toronto Press. This was only part of Jarvis's interest in the design of all the Gallery's printed material. He appointed Paul Arthur as Publications Officer. A Canadian typographic designer who had studied and worked in Switzerland, Arthur designed a format for the catalogues in which each work was illustrated and the component parts (biographical information, description of the work, literature, exhibitions, and provenance) were organized with great typographical clarity. As a result the catalogues represent standards of both scholarly and typographical excellence.

A further example of Jarvis's concern for the systematic documentation of the collection was his appointment of Nathan Stolow as Chief of Conservation and Scientific Research. Stolow, who is a Canadian with a Ph.D. in Conservation from the University of London, was encouraged to do research on the nature of artists' materials as well as to supervise the documentation of the physical state of the collection.

It would be misleading to suggest that Jarvis's primary interest was in the scholarly examination of the past, for he was encouragingly involved with the present. His appointment of Arthur was characteristic of his interest in contemporary design, and so was his strong support of the Design Centre, which had been established in McCurry's time. One of Jarvis's greatest pleasures was visiting artists' studios as he travelled from coast to coast. Artists from one end of the country to the other were given a feeling that the National Gallery was concerned with their welfare. Jarvis responded with particular enthusiasm to the work of Harold Town, Jacques de Tonnancour, and Gordon Smith, among others, and in the years he was Director the Gallery for the first time bought the work of Edmund Alleyn, Maxwell Bates, Suzanne Bergeron, Graham Coughtry, Jacques Dallaire, Roy Kiyooka, John Korner, Fernand Leduc, Jean-Paul Lemieux, Kenneth Lochhead, Jean-Paul Mousseau, Kazuo Nakamura, Takao Tanabe, Gordon Smith, Town and Tony Urquhart. Often these works were bought from the Gallery's own biennial exhibitions of

Canadian art or from exhibitions being sent abroad.

The pride Jarvis showed in the painting and sculpture of living Canadian artists also extended to Canada's past. He was convinced of the importance of David Milne, who had died in 1953. The Gallery mounted a memorial exhibition of Milne's watercolours and oils in 1955, the year Jarvis was appointed; it acquired eighteen Milnes at that time. In the *Annual Report* for 1955–6 Jarvis wrote: 'The largest number [of acquisitions] by one artist was a group by David Milne (1882–1953), the sensitive and very personal painter whose style so greatly differed from the norm of the period that he was all but overlooked during most of his life.' There were also other significant Canadian purchases. Five important examples of the work of James Wilson Morrice, including *Olympia* (plate 121), were bought out of the interest of the Associate Director, Donald Buchanan, who had written the standard biography of this painter. Within one fiscal year, 1957–8, some of the public's favourites in the Canadian collection were acquired on the recommendation of the Chief Curator, R. H. Hubbard: an anonymous nineteenth-century painting of *Micmac Indians*, Robert Todd's *The Ice Cone, Montmorency Falls* (plate 107), William Raphael's *Behind Bonsecours Market, Montreal* (plate 110), and Robert Harris's *Harmony* (plate 114). The *Still Life* by Ozias Leduc (plate XXV) had been bought the year Jarvis was appointed.

Of the non-Canadian purchases initiated in the Jarvis years, the most distinguished arose out of Jarvis's interest in modern sculpture. In 1955 the Gallery had very little beyond three Epstein bronzes and the Maillol acquired from the Vollard heirs. From the estate of Curt Valentin, the brilliant New York dealer, Jarvis bought (for the unbelievably small sum of $8,500) a marble Arp of 1938, a Lipchitz limestone of 1917 (plate 63), a Despiau bronze of 1918, a Matisse head of 1927, and a small Gerhard Marcks, as well as two drawings by Klee and Picasso. From Nathan in Zurich he acquired a superb early cast of Rodin's *The Age of Bronze*, in Paris a small Giacometti head, and from an English collector Henry Moore's *Reclining Woman* (plate 90). He bought from the sculptors themselves a Zadkine bronze and *Rock Drill* by Epstein (plate 86). The acquisition of all these works of sculpture, which were purchased for pennies, was Jarvis's greatest contribution to the collection.

Jarvis's sense of loyalty to the contributions of Brown, Beaverbrook, and Massey to the Gallery's collection of English pictures made it inevitable that he continue to build upon this undoubted strength, which he could do with the experience of fourteen years in England behind him. He asked the Trustees to appoint Philip James, then with the Arts Council in Great Britain, as a consultant. The Gallery spent very little money but added paintings by artists like Ceri Richards, Victor Pasmore, and William Scott to the collection. The work in this group that seems most impressive now is Francis Bacon's *Study for Portrait No. 7* (plate 92), which Jarvis bought in 1957 on Philip James's advice.

Jarvis was, in fact, concentrating upon the twentieth century. Although American abstract expressionism was at its height in the mid-fifties, the Trustees in May 1956 confirmed an unwritten policy against the collecting of contemporary American art that reflected (besides a possible touch of anti-Americanism) their belief that American works of art were easily accessible to Canadians in American galleries. They did, however, add a water-colour by Sam Francis the next year. In modern European art Jarvis also bought Chagall, a handsome Derain of 1912, Dufy, Marquet, Nicolas de Staël, Vuillard, Appel, and Severini. He ventured into the nineteenth century only to purchase a Puvis de Chavannes and a Pissarro pastel. His greatest successes in the acquisition of French paintings were the purchases of the Gallery's first paintings by Picasso – a large pastel synthetic Cubist work of 1919 (plate 64) – and Matisse – a nude of 1926 that legend has it Matisse himself chose for Ottawa (plate 65). In these purchases there was the influence of Donald Buchanan, Jarvis's Associate Director, who had become interested in French painting through his research on Morrice. And certainly Hubbard, as Chief Curator, was actively involved.

In the field of earlier European acquisitions, there was a portrait of *Lady Thynne* (plate 66) by the English seventeenth-century painter Cornelius Johnson, which the Gallery was fortunate enough to be given by the son and daughter of Paul Oppé in their father's memory. The Gallery bought a lime-stone late-French-Gothic *Madonna and Child* (plate 1) at Jarvis's instigation and paintings by Isaac Ouwater, Gawen Hamilton, and Joseph Wright of Derby. The most important acquisition, however, may have been Vouet's *The Fortune Teller* (plate 32), on the advice of Charles Sterling (from 1956 to 1959 an adviser to the Gallery), and Rossetti's attractive *Salutatio Beatricis* (plate 78), recommended by the Chief Curator. At the same time Miss Fenwick was buying major prints: in 1957, for example, Dürer's *Adam and Eve* and Rembrandt's *Hundred Guilder Print*. At Jarvis's suggestion Mr Joseph Hirshhorn made it possible for the Gallery to acquire Dürer's drawing, *Nude Woman with a Staff* (plate 158). Encouraged by the Chairman, Percy Fell, Jarvis made the first additions to the oriental collection in forty-three years. The Trustees gave him the authority to select three Chinese scrolls from an exhibition at the Royal Ontario Museum; one was the particularly fine painting given to Ch'iu Ying (plate 185). In none of these purchases was a large sum of money involved.

One of the reasons for the modesty of the acquisitions was undoubtedly that Jarvis and the Trustees were placing an emphasis on the program of the Gallery rather than on its collection. W. G. Constable's second report on the Gallery for the Trustees in 1956 (the first had been in 1931), which is remarkable for its sympathetic understanding of the Canadian situation, was primarily concerned with the Gallery's national responsibility to explain and interpret works of art to the general public. In the *Annual Report* for 1957–8 the Chairman of the Board pointed out that 'The report which follows places much of its emphasis on the educational and extension activities of the National Gallery.' It now seems clear that this is where Jarvis was placing his personal emphasis. Whereas the acquisition budget dropped from $920,371 in Jarvis's first year on the job (when the last group of Liechtenstein purchases were bought) to the surprisingly low sum of $25,000 in his last, the program and administration budget in those same years nevertheless rose from $260,830 to $722,981.

Unhappily Jarvis's many successful accomplishments as Gallery Director were clouded by an unsympathetic response on the part of politicians. Fundamentally this grew out of differences between Jarvis and the whole machinery of the government. He remembers with great affection the two Ministers of Citizenship and Immigration to whom he reported: J. W. Pickersgill for the Liberal government until 1957, who had insisted that the Gallery be moved from its antiquated space in the Victoria Museum – even if only into the temporary quarters of the newly constructed Lorne Building – and from 1957 the Hon. Ellen L. Fairclough for the Conservative Government, who saw Jarvis sympathetically through his resignation in 1959. But he was clearly an alien if exotic figure in the Ottawa bureaucracy.

From the beginning of Jarvis's appointment there were hints of the multiple problems that would make his stay at the National Gallery so short. One was the reaction of some columnists to his credentials. In spite of the apparent advantage of his having been a Rhodes scholar and a special assistant to Sir Stafford Cripps during the war, there were two faintly expressed suspicions of him: one that he might be somewhat of a dilettante, the other that he had lived in England too long (fourteen years). The average Canadian feared the snob. This was echoed in a House of Commons debate on 22 March 1956 when one member said:

The national gallery has a new director. I understand that Mr Jarvis is an extremely capable man. Sometimes he likes to make speeches. Down in Montreal a few weeks ago he was apparently rather disdainful about hardware merchants and others who take it upon themselves to criticize expenditures for art. There may be some justification for his disdain and certainly he is entitled to his opinion. But I would remind Mr Jarvis that it is the people of the constituency I represent and others, who have to pay the bills for these paintings. Indeed it is these people who pay his salary.

Another problem for Jarvis was that he had to finish the negotiations for the final group of Liechtenstein pictures to which his Board was committed. Admittedly he received a certain amount of kudos for the acquisition of the Simone Martini, the Chardins, and the Rubens, but he was also held responsible for the price. In the first Liechtenstein purchase of 1953 the two exquisite Filippino Lippis had been bought for $118,000 and the Rembrandt *Esther* for $158,000 – the largest sums the Gallery had ever paid – but the country was acquiring two early Renaissance works and a painting by an artist whose name was a household word everywhere in Canada. In 1954 the next group – four small northern masterpieces and the Guardi – had been bought for $363,000, or an average of about $55,000 each, a most reasonable figure for works of that quality. But now two years later, in 1956, four pictures from the same collection cost $850,000, or over $200,000 each. This was difficult to explain because the Rubens did not have the importance of the Rembrandt, and the name of Simone Martini was hardly known in Canada. The explanation for the prices was, of course, that private collectors were becoming active buyers again and that these small works could have attracted American collectors like Mr Charles Wrightsman and Mr Norton Simon. Parliament approved the purchase but never gave Jarvis as much money for regular acquisitions as it gave McCurry. In fact in Jarvis's time the purchase budget fell to the lowest point since the Second World War.

Another difficulty for Jarvis became apparent in the debate in the House about the Liechtenstein purchase. It is possible that no one from the Gallery took it sufficiently seriously when a member from Prince Albert, Saskatchewan, said in the House on 22 March 1956: 'With all due regard to the benefits that flow from viewing art for art's sake and pictures that are painted outside our country, I feel that first and foremost the national gallery in the capital city should be one to encourage, develop and expand Canadian art.' The member was John Diefenbaker, who was to lead the Conservative party to a narrow margin of victory over the Liberals in 1957; when he became Prime Minister he was already skeptical of the Gallery and its management, in spite of the fact that the Gallery had always bought and was continuing to buy Canadian works.

In this atmosphere of growing government suspicion Jarvis was not helped by the increasing complexity of the Board, the staff, and the system of advisers. Mr Fell was a democratic Chairman who gave the members of the Board (whose number had been increased to nine in 1952) a greater voice in the administration of the Gallery than Walker, Shepherd, Massey, or Southam had done. In addition three members of Jarvis's staff, as well as Jarvis himself, attended board meetings regularly: the Business Manager as secretary, and the Associate Director and Chief Curator by invitation. Finally, during his five years as director Jarvis had five external advisers: Constable, Blunt and Paul Oppé, whom he had inherited from McCurry, and Charles Sterling of the Louvre and Philip James whom the Board had appointed at his recommendation. The very diversity of opinions represented in the Board and. to the Board greatly diminished the unity, and therefore the strong support, that a relatively inexperienced museum director needed.

The Board had been led by the Liberal government, before its fall in 1957, to believe that another $400,000 would be available for the purchase of further Liechtenstein pictures. Before the election of that year Jarvis and his Curators had found two paintings they wanted to recommend to the government. One was a Liechtenstein picture, a small *Virgin of the Annunciation* by Lorenzo Monaco, which would add to the collection an important work of the early Italian Renaissance, a period W. G. Constable had told the Trustees in his 1956 report the Gallery had neglected. The other was a Pieter Brueghel the Elder which belonged to the Count von Pölnitz in Bavaria. This *Landscape with Christ Appearing to the Apostles* was, as the Board was told, the last Brueghel in private hands and would provide an important transition for the collection between Quentin Matsys and Rubens; it was also a large and expressive landscape painting.

The Board recommended the acquisition of these two works to the government. Then a situation arose that is almost impossible to disentangle and analyse. It has probably been best explained in the House on 12 March 1959 by the Leader of the Opposition, Lester B. Pearson (who was to become Prime Minister in 1963):

I have had the opportunity of making some investigation into this matter and . . . it is a confused, unhappy situation which brings no credit to the government and which, on the contrary, has resulted in a good deal of discredit . . . to the name of Canada in those circles which are concerned with art. . . .

As I understand the situation, the first contact between a representative of the gallery and the agent for the owner of the picture, a landscape by Breughel, was made *on January 4, 1957 . . . a value of approximately $500,000 was placed on the picture by the European owner.*

A good many months later, on October 22, 1957, after the election of that year, I believe the owner of the picture or the agent of the owner was informed that the trustees of the National Gallery, who would naturally have to pass on any purchase of a picture of this kind or any other kind, were interested. . . .

[The Gallery approached the cabinet for authority.] I gather . . . that the government got their information as to the availability of funds for this picture not from any treasury board authority, not from the Department of Finance, but from the officers of the National Gallery, from the director and trustees of the National Gallery. . . . On the basis of that information the cabinet on May 2, 1958 authorized the Acting Minister of Citizenship and Immigration to give permission to the director to proceed accordingly . . . with the negotiations for the purchase of the picture.

I am informed that the agent for the owner was told by the director of the gallery that he was authorized . . . to make an offer of $350,000 for this picture . . . without any strings attached, with payment to be made on delivery of the picture some time after May 12. . . . The owner accepted the offer and the agent wired the director of the gallery accordingly and requested, I am informed, written confirmation. . . .

[On May 8] the director, after all these negotiations had been completed, informed the agent that there would be difficulty in regard to the financing of this picture because the cabinet had authorized this firm offer on the understanding that the money was readily available from some fund which was in existence for the purchase of pictures from the Liechtenstein collection. Now they discovered, after this firm offer had been made, that there was no such money readily available from that fund. The agent was informed that it was hoped this difficulty would soon be cleared up and the contract could be signed.

It was not until four or five days after that, on May 12 or May 13, that finally the agent for the owner of this picture was able to see the minister concerned and the minister then explained that this was all very unfortunate; that there had been a misunderstanding; that the money which was thought to be available was not available and therefore the deal, if I may put it this way, was off and no purchase would be made.

It is possible that this speech, which was made almost a year after the purchase had been refused, was an attempt through discussion in the House to make the government reconsider its decision. But at no time could Jarvis or his Board muster enough support in Parliament – or, perhaps even more significantly, with the mandarins of the public service – to persuade the government to stand behind a cabinet mistake, let alone make an important acquisition for the National Gallery. On 1 July, some three months after Pearson's speech, the Chairman resigned, on 1 October the Director, and the next day Cleveland Morgan, one of the most discriminating members of the Board.

It is safe to say that, much as it may have been wished and even engineered in certain circles in Ottawa, the departure of no Director was as deeply mourned as Alan Jarvis's. In many respects his five years in office had seemed euphoric, and he left a martyr.

8 1960–1965
The Search for Stability

As a successor to Alan Jarvis a Director was sought who was unlikely to put the Conservative government in an embarrassing position. They found him in Charles Comfort, a man of admirable propriety. The Trustees announced his appointment in February 1960: 'Dr Comfort, an artist of established reputation [plate 141], came from the University of Toronto where he was Associate Professor in the Department of Art and Archaeology, an appointment he filled since 1938. During the war he served as an official war artist with the Canadian army with the rank of major, and at the time of his appointment he was President of the Royal Canadian Academy of Arts.'

Charles Comfort was a painter of considerable achievement whose finest works record the world of the Depression that recent generations have preferred to forget. He had also been a sound teacher of painting and the techniques of painting for the historians of art who went to his classes in the Studio Building where A.Y. Jackson was still painting. As a professor in Canada's first developed department of the history of art he was in a position to look expectantly to the young to fill the openings at the National Gallery; his assistant director from 1961 and his successor had been among his students.

Comfort's situation, as he himself realized in taking the appointment, was by no means enviable. It is recorded that at his first meeting with the Trustees 'Dr Comfort said that he regarded his acceptance of the position as a moral obligation and that he had accepted with certain reservations.' He not only had to re-establish a sense of confidence in the Gallery after the Breughel-Lorenzo Monaco débâcle but had to adjust to a new building that was opened just at the time he was appointed. The dreams of over fifty years were being half realized in the adaptation of an office building to a National Gallery which, although it had eight low-ceilinged storeys above ground and two below, was at least the National Gallery's own and was provided with de-

55

sirable temperature and humidity control. The decision to convert this building as it was being constructed had been made at the end of McCurry's
directorship; the plans were worked out in Jarvis's time; the exhausting move
of works of art, books, and people had been engineered by Donald Buchanan
as Acting Director. But it was Comfort's problem to break it in, with the
responsibility of satisfying the greater expectations of the public. He worked
at the task with characteristic seriousness and in June 1960 reported to the
Trustees: 'Whether I have brought wisdom to my decisions still remains
to be proven, but the effort has been to maintain the normal planned activities
of the National Gallery at the level of maximum usefulness, inspiration, and
efficiency in the interest of the Canadian public.'

Comfort also had to stabilize (and enlarge) a staff that had been disturbed
by the transition from the great hopes of Jarvis's régime to his resignation.
A further complication came with the resignation of Jarvis's eccentric and
endearing Associate Director, Donald Buchanan. He had been active with
McCurry in founding the National Industrial Design Council in 1948, the
Canadian Film Institute, and the magazine *Canadian Art*, which he edited
from 1944 to 1959 – all of which received Jarvis's unqualified support – and
remained as Acting Director to supervise the move. But he resigned shortly
after Comfort took over as Director; three years later he was made a Trustee.
His loss was felt keenly since he had been responsible for the Gallery's activities
abroad and had supervised the building in 1958 of the Canadian Pavilion at
the Venice Biennale.

In Buchanan's place Comfort brought back to the Gallery as Assistant
Director one of his former students, Dr William S. A. Dale, in whose judge-
ment he placed great confidence. At the same time he reported to the Trustees
of his consciousness of the value of the continuing support of the Chief
Curator, Dr Hubbard. With one staff member hired by Jarvis, Dr Nathan
Stolow, he shared an interest in the scientific analysis of works of art; he gave
Stolow full support in building up a National Conservation Research Labora-
tory that has received international recognition.

Comfort attached great importance to enlarging the collection. In accept-
ing the position of Director he stated that he 'wished to be assured of adequate
funds for the purchase of works of art'. He was given an average of slightly
over $200,000 a year, which could be considered 'adequate' but not generous
with the rising market. He was, of course, very much interested in the
acquisition of Canadian art. In the 1962–3 *Annual Report* it was stated that
'the Trustees feel that major works by Canadian artists of the present day
should be added to the collection whenever possible, to match the achieve-

ments of the past and set standards for the future. Into this category falls the monumental canvas *3+4+1* [plate XXXII] by Paul-Émile Borduas (1905–1960), which was the keystone of the artist's memorial exhibition in 1962.' A major purchase from a living artist was Riopelle's large *Pavane* in 1963. Among the acquisitions of earlier Canadian works were the purchases of the anonymous Canadian primitive portrait of *Mrs Charles Morrison* (plate 105) and the wooden *Angel* by François-Noël Levasseur (plate 100) and two gifts: the quaint polychrome *St Luke* by Urbain Brien (dit Desrochers) from Mrs Nettie Sharp, St Lambert, Québec; and the graceful silver *Madonna* (plate 104) by Salomon Marion given by E. E. Poole of Edmonton.

English art continued to attract the Gallery. Works by artists like Alan Davie and Peter Lanyon were added to the twentieth-century collection. At the same time this part of the collection was given a new character by Dr Hubbard's preoccupation with Victorian art, which grew out of his preparation for an exhibition called 'Victorian Artists in England' in the spring of 1965. Purchases were made of paintings by William Powell Frith, James Collinson, James Tissot, Abraham Solomon (plate 76), John Linnell, and Augustus Egg. An attractive addition to the earlier British collection was Raeburn's *Portrait of Jacobina Copland* (plate 73).

For the first time there was an interest in early American art, expressed in the purchase of Robert Henri's *Portrait of George Luks* (plate 94) and a still-life by William M. Harnett. These two American pictures filled 'a long-standing lack in the collection', in the words of the *Report* of 1961–2. 'Before the purchase . . . the Gallery had nothing of importance from American painting of the late nineteenth century, a period when it greatly influenced Canadian art.' The Gallery was also fortunate to receive an eighteenth-century American conversation piece from Jasper H. Nicolls of Ottawa, *The Tannatt Family* by Henry Benbridge (plate 93). This gift had been encouraged by the Curator of Canadian art, J. R. Harper.

While the Gallery continued to ignore contemporary American art, it did buy paintings by Manessier, Feito, and Otto Piene and sculpture by Ipousteguy, Marini, and – in the interregnum between directors – Manzù and Barbara Hepworth.

The virtue of acquiring sculpture, which had been demonstrated in the acquisition of Canadian and contemporary pieces, was also seen as desirable for the traditional European collection, in particular by the Chief Curator. One purchase was an interesting fifteenth-century *Virgin and Child* by the Master of the Marble Madonnas. Another piece, which was described in the *Annual Report* of 1965–6 as a 'work of great rarity and beauty', was a *Virgin and Child*, then attributed to Veit Stoss. In its fascination with polychromy the Gallery, after the retirement of Dr Comfort, bought an eighteenth-century Austrian *Tobias and the Angel* in which the silver, gold, and colours are in impeccable condition still.

In this period it is difficult to establish a pattern in the European acquisitions. They began with the disappointing purchase of a *St Jerome* thought to be by Georges de la Tour, but which was actually by Trophime Bigot, and, simultaneously, the commendable one of Jan Steen's *The Lean Kitchen* (plate 30). A most attractive addition to the Italian Renaissance collection was Catena's *Holy Family in a Landscape* (plate 11), bought from Agnew. Perhaps in reaction to the sobriety of the rest of the collection, works were often acquired that were decorative, like Jan Brueghel's *Bouquet of Flowers*; or small, feminine, and charming, like Louis Boilly's *Portrait of a Young Woman*; or elegant, like David's oval *Portrait of M. Sériziat*. The most important single purchase from a dealer while Comfort was still Director was probably Dosso Dossi's *Aeneas at the Entrance of the Elysian Fields* (plate 12), a sensual landscape painting that greatly enriches the sixteenth-century collection.

Comfort and the Trustees rightly encouraged the activities of the Curator of Prints and Drawings, Miss Fenwick, who bought three important English drawings: Romney's *Dido Bidding Farewell to Aeneas* (plate 181), Millais's charming *The Return of the Dove to the Ark* (plate 183), and Augustus John's *Dorelia in the Black Hat* (plate 184). To the German expressionist drawings she had been acquiring, she added Kirchner's *Portrait of a Woman* (plate 176) of 1906, and to the French collection, Matisse's *Young Woman in a Mantilla*. She bought at least three master prints during this time: Dürer's engraving of *St Eustace*, Bellange's etching of *The Adoration of the Magi*, and Edvard Munch's colour woodcut, *Evening: Melancholy on the Beach*. In 1960 Mr A. E. Popham, who had retired as Keeper at the British Museum, was appointed as an adviser on drawings; his most significant purchase for the Gallery during these years was the Italian drawing, *Nine Famous Men* (plate 156). The fourth catalogue of the permanent collection appeared in 1965 as a result of the co-operation of Mr Popham (essentially the editor) and Miss Fenwick; this was *European Drawings in the Collection of the National Gallery of Canada*.

Although there were still other purchases, like the Jacopo di Cione triptych and Marquet's particularly fine *Paris in the Snow*, this might have gone down as one of the least adventurous periods in the history of the Gallery's acquisitions if there had not been at the end of it a decision to apply to the government for special appropriations to bid at the Spencer-Churchill sale at Christie's in April 1965. At that sale the Gallery acquired two energetic

Italian baroque works. The more dramatic is Orazio Gentileschi's *Lot and his Daughters* (plate XI); but Guercino's *Christ and the Woman of Samaria* (plate 18), although a later work, has great presence in the collection. A third acquisition at the sale was the work then called *Education of the Prince* (*Young Cavalier Executing a Passade . . .*, plate 23) by Jacob Jordaens. This seemed a pleasant baroque conceit in relation to the education of mankind symbolized in Piero di Cosimo's *Vulcan and Aeolus*, which had been in the Gallery for almost thirty years. The Gentileschi, Guercino, and Jordaens cost $393,095.

Charles Comfort was a conscientious Director who above all was intent upon restoring to the Gallery a sense of security. It is good to be able to record that when he retired from the Gallery in July 1965, the three Spencer-Churchill pictures had been triumphantly acquired the month before.

9 1966 and after

I came to the Gallery one year after Charles Comfort retired; in the meantime Dr William S. A. Dale had been Acting Director. On 4 May 1966 my appointment was announced in the House of Commons by the Secretary of State, Judy LaMarsh:

MR SPEAKER: *I am pleased to inform the House that the Civil Service Commission has approved the appointment of Dr Jean Sutherland Boggs as Director of the National Gallery of Canada. Her appointment also has the unanimous support of the Board of Trustees of the Gallery. . . .*

Miss Boggs, who is a Canadian, is a graduate of the University of Toronto in Fine Art and of Radcliffe College at Harvard University, where she obtained her Doctorate. From 1948 to 1962 she was employed as an Assistant and Associate Professor of Art at three institutions in the United States – Skidmore College, Mount Holyoke College, and the University of California.

In 1962 Miss Boggs was appointed Curator of the Art Gallery of Toronto. During the succeeding two years she was instrumental in the organization of several major exhibitions at the Toronto Gallery, among them the highly successful one on 'Picasso and Man'. Miss Boggs left Toronto in 1964 to take up the Steinberg Professorship at Washington University, the first to be established on this continent for the study of modern art.

I think all Canadians interested in the development of the Gallery and the furtherance of our cultural life in general will be pleased at the appointment of a Canadian of such national and international stature. For my own part, I need hardly add that I am particularly happy to see a woman filling such a senior position among our cultural agencies. She is, in fact, the first woman to head an agency with the status of Deputy Minister.

The most crucial change in the Gallery since then had to do with legislation that became law on 1 April 1968: the Gallery was placed, along with three other national museums (the National Museum of Natural Sciences, the National Museum of Man, the National Museum of Science and Technology), under a single board, with a Secretary-General responsible for financial and certain administrative matters. The purpose, as stated by the minister, Miss LaMarsh, in defending the Act in the House, was administrative simplicity and economy and the hope of freeing the Directors for 'their professional responsibilities'. When the Gallery's Trustees under M. Jean Raymond, who had been their Chairman since 1964, protested that 'the National Gallery will be submerged in the complexity of a corporation of museums with different functions; its role as a national gallery with a truly national purpose could be lost', the Prime Minister assured them that a special committee could be set up for the Gallery. The result is a Visiting Committee. It has been entrusted by the Board (whose Chairman is Jean Ostiguy of Montreal) with the power to approve the aquisition of any work costing less than $100,000, and its recommendations for purchases over that sum are given the most serious consideration. Under its first Chairman, Mr J. R. Longstaffe of Vancouver, and his successor, Professor G. S. Vickers of Toronto, this committee has shown deep concern for the maintenance of the quality of the collection.

The Visiting Committee has been interested in increasing the scope of the Gallery's collection beyond the classic limits of a National Gallery – into the decorative arts; further into the past than the Renaissance; and into the world beyond Europe and America. So far this interest has had to be theoretical, although one of the committee's members, Mr R. W. Finlayson of Toronto, has in fact for five years been giving paintings by the eighteenth-century Chinese eccentrics (plate 186). A further impetus to widening the range of the collection so that it might become a Museum of Fine Arts is provided by scruples on the part of French-speaking Canadians over the commercial implications of the word 'Galerie' in the traditional French version of the Gallery's name: la Galerie nationale du Canada. The Committee and the Board feel, however, that a change in the character of the collection is desirable to justify a change of name. As a result the collection may well develop beyond its present scope.

Perhaps the most radical change in acquisition policy has been the decision to buy contemporary American art. The Trustees revoked its former policy and the Public Service Commission appointed as Curator of Contemporary Art Mr Brydon Smith, who has organized at the Gallery two superbly installed exhibitions of the work of American artists, James Rosenquist in 1968 and Dan Flavin in 1969. Works were bought by Rosenquist (plate 97) and Flavin and by other artists such as Jules Olitski, George Segal (plate 99), Tony Smith,

61

Carl Andre, and Nancy Graves. In addition two 'old masters' of the post-war period were acquired: Jackson Pollock's *No. 29, 1950* (plate XXXI) and David Smith's *Wagon I* of 1963–4 (plate 98). An American summer resident of Saint Andrews, New Brunswick, Mrs E. F. Eidlitz, gave the small collection more substance by adding oils by Arthur Dove (plate 95) and Lyonel Feininger (plate 96) and a small gouache by Charles Sheeler.

Since I spent so many years in the United States it may be thought that I have been Americanizing the collection. But the twentieth century seemed so tame – even with its Cubist Picasso (plate 64), its solid Matisse (plate 65), its three Fauve landscapes – that my compulsion was to enliven it with some of the energy that has been associated with the United States in at least the first half of the century. As a result we even bought paintings by two Europeans who loved New York: Fernand Léger's *The Mechanic* (plate XXIX), which was painted long before he crossed the Atlantic, and Mondrian's *Composition with Blue Square* (plate XXX), which was actually finished there in 1942. Other European works with no American links also provided that decisiveness and energy that I felt the Gallery needed. *Les Deux filles* by Rouault (plate 60) has a certain acknowledgement of reality that the collection lacked, and this was happily complemented by a gift from Mr Hamilton Southam of a *Crucifixion* by the same artist, so that we can now show his awareness of both sin and redemption. Another work that gave the collection greater vitality was Van Dongen's *Souvenir de la saison de l'Opéra russe* 1909 (plate 61), which the Chief Curator found at Dubourg, Paris, in 1966.

We have continued to buy contemporary Canadian works and sponsor exhibitions of the work of living Canadian artists abroad. For this reason, and because the most unconventional works are often shown on the Gallery's ground floor – which, with its glass walls, is dramatically visible from the street – we are often accused of, or complimented on, being a museum of modern art. But the National Gallery is as much a historical museum as it was in the time of Walker and Brown. We buy modern art in the hope – even on the gamble – that it will represent our time for the future. The Gallery was freed from a sense of obligation to be the sole patron of young Canadian painters by the establishment of the Canada Council in 1957; as a result we can buy with conviction the work of an artist we feel has already proved himself. Some clue to the Gallery's interests can be found in its exhibitions of Canadian art abroad: Molinari and Comtois at the Venice Biennale of 1968 and Michael Snow in 1970; Jack Bush and Hurtubise at the São Paulo Bienal in 1957 and Greg Curnoe, Robert Murray, and Iain Baxter in 1969. Both Molinari and Robert Murray have won prizes. In more comprehensive exhibitions like 'Canada: Art d'aujourd'hui', which was shown in Paris, Rome, Brussels, and Lausanne in 1968, or in 'Eight Artists from Canada' at Tel-Aviv in 1970, more established painters like Riopelle and Alex Colville have been included as well as Claude Tousignant, Charles Gagnon, and Joyce Wieland. There are others whom the Gallery admires, and whose work it is buying, but to whom it has not as yet given emphasis abroad.

With the intensified historicism of contemporary life we often 'fill gaps' in the Canadian collection in the hope that the quality justifies the acquisition. Thus we have bought the work of artists hitherto ignored, like Bertram Brooker (plate 137), or works from periods we have neglected in the careers of living artists like Lawren Harris (plate 136) or Guido Molinari (plate 146). With the tolerance of the young, curators Pierre Théberge and Dennis Reid, who are particularly close to artists now working in Canada, have added works by earlier artists such as Horatio Walker and Suzor-Côté. Among the interesting early paintings Théberge has found is *L'Enfant au pain* by Ozias Leduc (plate 117). The scholarly interest in Canadian art, which was established at the Gallery by two former curators of this material, R.H. Hubbard and J.R. Harper, has been developed by the younger generation, which includes Reid, Théberge, and in particular Jean-René Ostiguy as Research Curator. It should be further enhanced by the appointment of Jean Trudel as Curator of Early Canadian Art, appropriately at a time when the government has acquired the William H. Coverdale Collection of Canadiana for the Public Archives and the Gallery. In preparing exhibitions this staff has been encouraged to do exhaustive research on the works in the collection. The investigation of Dennis Reid, for example, on the Gallery's Morrices for an exhibition of this artist's work held in France and England in 1968 and his publication of the catalogue of the Group of Seven for the exhibition he arranged to commemorate the fiftieth anniversary of the Group's first exhibition, provide an important contribution to our knowledge of Canadian art and will make the next edition of the catalogue of the *Canadian School* (Volume III) more exhaustive.

Within this period there have been two important gifts that have been the result of their donors' long associations with the Gallery. One was the thoughtful bequest of the late Vincent Massey of all the paintings the Gallery chose to select from his collection; as a result almost 100 Canadian works were acquired, including an important Comfort (plate 141) and a Krieghoff (plate 109). In the Massey bequest there was also a large group of works by David Milne. The Milne collection was further increased by the 225 Milnes included in the gift of Mrs J.P. Barwick, comprising almost 700 works from the estate of her brother, Douglas M. Duncan. This has been the largest gift in the Gallery's history and means a great deal as the record of the collecting of Duncan, one of the most endearing figures in the world of Canadian art. The 170 Milne dry-points that Duncan had always promised Miss Fenwick for the Gallery are of particular significance.

In addition to the acquisition of American art, there has been another departure: the building of a collection of photography. James Borcoman, the former head of the Education Department, became its Acting Curator and finally in 1970 its full-time Curator. After discussions with the Public Archives and the National Film Board, which also collect photographs, it was decided that the National Gallery should specialize in photographs considered to be works of art outside Canada. The most important acquisition in the four years of the collection's existence (with a total budget for those years of $30,000) may be the 106 photographs by the mid-nineteenth-century French photographer Charles Nègre (plate 187), which appear to form the largest group of his work in America. Part of the collection has formed an exhibition called 'The Photograph as Object', which has circulated throughout Canada.

It was in this period that Miss Fenwick retired. Her long tenure at the Gallery had been animated by her discrimination and charm. The first eighteen months I was director she selflessly worked on one of the Gallery's most important projects outside Ottawa: the Fine Arts Gallery at Expo 67 in Montreal. Donald Buchanan, when he was a Trustee of the Gallery, had persuaded the government of the need for such a gallery at the fair and had become its director. When he died in January 1966, Miss Fenwick took over from him. It was an opportunity for the Gallery to show its expertise in several directions. It had never had a full opportunity to demonstrate at Ottawa its knowledge of how to engineer a gallery to produce optimum conditions for the protection of works of art. With the guidance of the Gallery's Dr Nathan Stolow, a building with the ideal system of temperature and humidity control was constructed on the fair site. As a result, works of art that came from all over the world – from twenty-one countries – could be given perfect care. The paintings sent from Ottawa itself – its Piero di Cosimo, its Hobbema, its *Vegetable Market* by Canaletto, its *Pourvoyeuse* by Chardin – did not pale beside works borrowed from the Hermitage in Leningrad, the Rijksmuseum in Amsterdam, or the Louvre in Paris; we felt a genuine pride in them. The catalogue, *Man and his World*, was also important to the Gallery as an effort to bring to bear upon the works exhibited, in a way that would make them more comprehensible to the uninitiated visitor to the fair, the best scholarship of Canada and other countries. Miss Fenwick co-ordinated every step.

Happily during her last two years with the Gallery it was possible to give Miss Fenwick a large budget, which she spent on (among other things) Domenico Tiepolo's *Visiting Time at a Nunnery* (plate 167), Delacroix's pastel of the *Crucifixion* (plate 170), the great early drawing by Van Gogh, *The Swamp* (plate 173), and Matisse's *Dancer Resting* (plate 180). In 1969, to honour her achievements, the Gallery, in collaboration with the Department of External Affairs, held exhibitions of drawings from the collection in London (at Colnaghi, where many drawings had been bought with the sympathetic guidance of Mr James Byam Shaw), as well as at the Uffizi in Florence and at the Louvre. Critics in all three cities praised what she had accomplished with the help of her advisers, Paul Oppé and A. E. Popham. 'The drawings steadily acquired for Canada's National Gallery are of consistently fine quality and reflect breadth of view as well as discriminating judgement,' wrote William Gaunt in *The Times*. 'Preference has often been given to drawings that show minor masters at their best instead of those that would only indifferently represent great men.' Jean Bouret wrote in *Les Lettres Françaises* that 'la collection complète est d'une telle richesse qu'on aurait quelque raison d'être jaloux; mais comment être jaloux de ces gentils Canadiens si pleins de ferveur?'

Under Mary C. Taylor, her successor as Curator of Drawings, new research was done on these drawings and new material uncovered that should be a stimulus for an eventual revision of the catalogue of *European Drawings* (Volume IV). Since Miss Fenwick's retirement acquisitions have inevitably been slower, but one important drawing (much admired by the Louvre) has been added: the *St John the Baptist Preaching* by Jacques Bellange (plate 161), which adds considerable interest to the Northern Mannerist collection.

There are no longer official advisers to the collection, although there are a great many unofficial ones. Popham retired when Miss Fenwick did in 1968. But in addition to the Chief Curator and the Curator of European Art, Gyde Shepherd, it was felt desirable to have a research curator of European Art who would spend approximately half of each year abroad. Myron Laskin was appointed and has led us to, among other things, two Lombard fifteenth-century reliefs, and a terracotta *Madonna and Child* after Donatello in Florence, a Frans Hals (plate 27) in a private English collection, and a Klimt (plate XXVI) in Turin. He has also given advice, support, and even encouragement on the acquisition of other works he cannot claim to have discovered himself. One of these is Jordaens' *'As the Old Sing, So the Young Twitter'* (plate XIII). His research, abbetted by Shepherd and the documentation of the National Research Conservation Laboratory, will lead to revisions of

Volumes I and II of the catalogues of the permanent collection.

The Gallery's seventeenth-century collection has recently been enhanced by three important works. The first was bought with a special grant of $365,000 during Canada's centennial year: *The Tribute Money* by Rembrandt (plate 24) found in New York by the Chief Curator and Mr Shepherd, and, as I suggested to the press, an appropriate subject for the payment of the tax-payers' dollars. It is a small work, painted in Leyden in 1629 and therefore informative in relation to the *Esther* painted after Rembrandt arrived in Amsterdam. (Both have survived the reduction of Rembrandt's *oeuvre* by scholars that has taken place during the three-hundredth anniversary of his death.) Another small work is a restrained Frans Hals portrait (plate 27), the first in the collection. The third recent acquisition – Jordaens' '*As the Old Sing, So the Young Twitter*' – was shown in the exhibition of the work of this artist that was organized by Michael Jaffé around the Gallery's *Education of the Prince*, which Jaffé rechristened *Young Cavalier Executing a Passade in the Presence of Mercury and Mars* (plate 23). In this 1968 Jordaens exhibition, the largest ever held of this artist's work and surely also the most scholarly, '*As the Old Sing*' caused such a sensation by its very vulgarity and sensuality – qualities hitherto lacking in the collection – that it seemed irresistible to bid for it (through Agnew as agent) at Sotheby's in London shortly after the exhibition closed. It was bought for $211,560 and sent on a special tour of thirteen cities in Canada from Victoria to St John's, Newfoundland.

As the nineteenth-century collection was heavily balanced toward Courbet and Impressionism, the first paintings by Delacroix, Chassériau, and Gustave Moreau were bought to represent French Romanticism, which is now also illustrated in its later stages by the purchase of a large Carrière that Picasso had copied. Neoclassicism also entered the Gallery through a marble bust of *Josephine* by Chinard and a full-length figure of a *Dancer* by Canova (plate 42) that the Empress herself originally commissioned. The group of three pastels by Degas was varied by two oil portraits: an early interpretation of a Pontormo drawing in the Uffizi (plate 54), bought from the Toronto collector, R. W. Finlayson, and *Woman with an Umbrella* (plate XXIII), which was once owned by Arthur Sachs. Finally, to give substance to the mild paintings by Gauguin in the collection, we bought a *Head of Meyer de Haan* (plate 57) that he had carved and painted in Brittany either in 1889 or 1890.

In spite of these purchases, made with more generous annual appropriations than any previous Director had possessed, there is still much to be done. We now have the facilities to give our present collection the most intensive care – whether it comes from the knowledge, skill, and research of the National Conservation Research Laboratory or the scholarship of the curators. But we are not as yet in a position to present it effectively to the public. Although the European collection has been somewhat stabilized on the second floor of our eight-storey building, there is no room for expansion; when a new work is acquired, an old one must be withdrawn. This means that the level of the collection is constantly refined – more so, perhaps, than is desirable in a public museum. The exhibition of contemporary work in the small gallery space on the fifth floor is lively since it is frequently changed because of new acquisitions; but this means that nothing is seen in a historical perspective. The Canadian collection suffers the most serious deprivation, since it cannot be seen in any continuity. No single floor of the Gallery could provide enough space for an adequate survey of Canadian art, and in our present building it is divided among three floors. A new building is needed to present the collection intelligibly to the public and also to provide additional space where the arts could be explained by films, television, and photographic exhibitions.

While the collection needs to be made more comprehensible by the addition of space, the Gallery still must develop other ways of making it more meaningful. Before I was Director I gave two Canadian Broadcasting Corporation series called *Listening to Pictures*, which reached people throughout the country. We need the staff to produce such material regularly, whether through radio, television, films or publications.

Not only does the collection need to be interpreted. It must be expanded if the Gallery is to continue to be considered a national resource for exhibitions in outlying centres. In the twentieth-century collection there is no example of analytical Cubism, no Dadaism, no Surrealism, no German Expressionism (except in the Department of Prints and Drawings), no Modigliani, only a Fauve Braque, and no violent or sensual work by Picasso. The knowledge of these very omissions and the cost of reducing them provide the motives behind the Gallery's emphasis on buying contemporary art. In other periods, the eighteenth century needs more than the small group that surrounds the exquisite Liechtenstein Chardins. There could be a stronger representation of neoclassicism to explain West's *Death of Wolfe* and the *Dancer* by Canova; perhaps some day we might even buy an Ingres. The five Cézannes would be even more pleasurable with the addition of a superb still-life. There could be more sculpture throughout the collection – by Bernini, Puget, Lemoyne, Carpeaux. For historical reasons it would be satisfying if the group of seventeenth-century French pictures were larger and contained works by artists who have as much meaning for the French tradition in Canada as has Philippe de Champaigne. If the large English collection were enlivened by the acquisition of a female portrait by Gainsborough and a great landscape by Constable, it would offer even greater visual pleasure. Finally, the Italian collection established by Walker, Brown, and Ricketts would gain stature with a Lorenzo Monaco, a Bellini, a Lorenzo Lotto, or a Pontormo.

Let us hope that the National Gallery of Canada's is a young collection still.

The Plates

I Simone Martini

Siena 1280/5 – Avignon 1344

St Catherine, c. 1320

Tempera on panel, 32¾ × 16 in. (83.2 × 40.6 cm.)
No. 6430. Bought with Agnew as agent from the Prince of Liechtenstein, 1956.

For the early fourteenth century, which was just beginning to stir out of the Middle Ages, St Catherine represented a combination of chastity, conviction, and breeding that this age of chivalry could revere. According to tradition she was a virgin from a fourth-century aristocratic family of Alexandria (as we might guess from her crown and the exquisite embroidery on the garnet-red dress), who confounded scholars with her arguments for Christianity (hence the quilled pen in her left hand), and who was consequently tied to the wheel (symbolized by the brooch at her throat), which shattered at her touch. She was nevertheless finally martyred by a headsman's sword (which she holds in her right hand).

This small panel of *St Catherine* must have been part of a polyptych for a church altar, almost certainly painted by Simone Martini in Orvieto in 1320 following the pattern of another, painted the year before, that was dedicated to St Catherine for the church of the same name in Pisa. By then Simone had already painted the fresco of the *Maestà* in the Palazzo Pubblico in Siena and a large panel of St Louis of Toulouse crowning his brother King of Naples.

Simone's refinement in juxtaposing and tooling the ornament and disposing the colours against the traditional gold ground is a reminder that he was a painter in the Sienese tradition, influenced by Duccio who had died two years before, and revealing the indebtedness of Siena to Byzantium. His contours are as important as Duccio's but they are not drawn as independent lines and move more languorously and more suavely. Their very grace, which we feel in the hair and the neck as well as in St Catherine's garments, is contrasted with the brooding intensity with which the artist has transformed the traditional Byzantine features, partly with sculptural modelling and partly with shadow. This expressive quality was to become stronger and perhaps culminates in the famous *Annunciation* of 1333 on which both Simone and his brother-in-law, Lippo Memi, were to collaborate.

Simone, who was a close friend of Petrarch, died in exile with the Papal Court in Avignon.

II German School

Cologne or Westphalia

The Madonna of the Flowering Pea, early fifteenth century

Tempera on panel, $27\frac{1}{2} \times 19\frac{1}{4}$ in. (69.8 x 49 cm.)
No. 6088. Bought from van Wisselingh, Amsterdam, 1953

There has been some question about the identification of the painter of this Madonna and Child but none about his coming from a crucial period in the history of art and the history of ideas. The artist may have been somewhat naive in drawing the hands of the Virgin, her ears and her crown, or in relating the heads spatially to the haloes, but the pleasure he gives us in the medium of this badly crackled tempera panel reminds us that he was working in Germany at a time when an interest in medium and techniques was leading to the production of the first prints and ultimately (a little later than this painting) to the first printing. We relish the warmth of the glowing red cloak, the coolness of the lavender lining, the depth of the blue of the Madonna's dress, and the softness of the yellow of the hair and the gold ground against the pale flesh. We respect the sensitive handling of the Virgin's face and neck and are soothed by yielding contours that can lead us to the Infant's hands, which open up like the tendrils of a flower. Those pleading hands, the happy expectancy in his face and the infinite sadness of hers – even the chorus of small, slyly-knowing angels in the background – remind us of the inevitability of the Passion. This painting shows the German concern for religion as an expression of simple devotion at a time when the interests of the rest of Western Europe were apt to be more secular, or at least more complex.

III Hans Memling

Seligenstadt *c*.1433 – Bruges 1494

The Virgin and Child with St Anthony Abbot and a Donor, 1472

Oil on panel, 36½ × 21⅛ in. (92.7 × 53.7 cm.)
No. 6191. Bought with Agnew as agent from the Prince of Liechtenstein, 1954.

Hans Memling could easily have come from the same tradition as the painter of the *Madonna of the Flowering Pea* (plate II). About the time the latter was painting, Memling was born near Mainz on the Rhine. Something in the gentleness of the modelling and interpretation of this small panel of the Madonna and Child suggests that he could have been trained in Germany before he made his way to Bruges in Flanders.

By 1465, when Memling reached Bruges, which provided the kind of patronage represented by the kneeling figure with the open purse tied to his belt, he must have come under two principal influences: Jan van Eyck, long dead, and Roger van der Weyden, with whom Memling might actually have studied in Brussels before Roger died in 1464. In any case the lovingly painted interior of this room, the glimpse of the landscape through the window and door, the exacting description of the substance and surfaces of materials, and the light that binds the figures to an improbably small setting, are part of a tradition that Jan van Eyck had created and Roger had continued. (We can find 1472, the date he inscribed, high on the wall between canopy and window.) Memling's work, however, is less intense and more ritualistically (if more sweetly) devout. His figures observe all the courtesies of the courtly tradition; even the pig, a reminder of St Anthony's triumph over lust, is as domesticated as a dog. There may be echoes of the earlier painters in the clarity and angularity of the drawing of the hands and draperies, but on the whole Memling is a mellifluous painter. He plays on the possibilities of oil as a medium as he paints the light and shadow of the tiled floor or the window ledge or pulls out the warmth of the Virgin's red robe against the restrained respectability of the donor's plum-coloured garment or St Anthony's decent black. At the same time his figures are often melancholy, as they are here – perhaps, as is commonly suggested, in anticipation of the Passion but perhaps also in unconscious acknowledgement of the ultimate effect upon fifteenth-century values of the skepticism of the Renaissance in contemporary Italy.

IV Filippino Lippi

Florence 1457/8–1504

*Esther at the Palace Gate, c.*1474–80

Tempera on panel, 19¼ x 17 in. (49 x 43.2 cm.)
No. 6085. Bought with Schab as agent from the Prince of Liechtenstein, 1953.

Ottawa is fortunate in having two small panels from two cassones, or marriage chests, that were probably commissioned from Botticelli by a Florentine family but that were executed instead by his pupil and ward, Filippino Lippi. The narrative of one of the chests begins with the painting reproduced here. Esther, or Hadassah, whom Mordecai 'took for his own daughter' and who was 'fair and beautiful', approaches the king's house. In the far more complex and horizontal panel, now at Chantilly, she is shown with other maidens modestly brought before the king and leaving his presence with the dignity of the queen she was to become. In the third panel she goes out from the palace. On the second chest there is a scene of the mortification of Mordecai; another of his persuasion of the king and the hanging of his enemy; and, finally, the scene of the other Ottawa panel (plate 4) – his triumph.

Filippino Lippi, who was the son of Fra Filippi Lippi and perhaps not twenty when he painted this work, was less obviously under the influence of his teacher Botticelli than we might have expected. He painted the tender spring landscape freely, as if he did not admit the traditional restrictions of tempera as a medium. The slender tree is as graceful and as vulnerable as Esther herself. Whereas Filippino made the palace in Ottawa's other panel of Mordecai solid and convincingly scaled, these buildings are small and curiously related to each other as if he were suggesting that they were evoked by Esther's imagination. Esther's body has a mannered gracefulness but the skirt of her heavy rose dress trails the ground, suggesting her hesitations. Filippino's drawing of Esther's profile and of the elegantly and incredibly long fingers of her left hand, and his fluid painting of her softly golden hair, express her beauty and wonderment.

V Piero di Cosimo

Florence 1462–1521

Vulcan and Aeolus, c.1490

Oil on canvas, 61¼ x 65½ in. (155.6 x 166.4 cm.)
No. 4287. Bought from Schaeffer, New York, 1937.

In this large canvas we find a vision of the beginnings of civilization by one of the most eccentric artists living in one of the most complicated and self-conscious periods in the history of man: the Florentine Renaissance. In painting *Vulcan and Aeolus* Piero di Cosimo carried out a commission from a rich and republican merchant, Francesco del Pugliese, for a group of works based on the figure of Vulcan. The late Erwin Panofsky surmised that the patron found this god sympathetic as 'the only ungentlemanly workman in the Olympian leisure class'. It has even been suggested that the strong features of the stiff-legged Vulcan in the lower left of the painting are Pugliese's own.

For his patron Piero created a primordial and rocky nature. He filled this world with animal life: a moth on the plant in the lower right; a cricket on the stone in the foreground; large exotic birds in the sky; an ungainly and miniature camel; a couple of dogs; a magnificent giraffe. The giraffe is mentioned by Luca Landucci, a Florentine, in his diary for 11 November 1487: 'Certain animals . . . came from some good friends of Florence who hoped to be duly rewarded. The animals [included] a very tall giraffe, beautiful and graceful; her picture can be seen painted in many parts of Florence.'

Against this animated image of nature are the commanding figures of men and gods, supply modelled with long, slow contours and somewhat flattened by the later abrasion of the paint. One man sleeps, another wakens as he stretches his foot, while a mother passionately embraces her child. The rider of the white horse in the centre of the canvas, who leads a second brown horse, gazes down at Vulcan, who industriously continues to forge a horse-shoe while Aeolus looks up from his twin bellows. Carpenters in the background build a hut according to the descriptions of primitive architecture by the Roman architect Vitruvius. The painting seems an innocent wish for a time when man was simple and young.

VI Quentin Matsys

Louvain 1465/6 – Antwerp 1530

*The Crucifixion, c.*1520

Oil on arched panel, 20⅛ x 14⅜ in. (51 x 36.5 cm.)
No. 6190. Bought with Agnew as agent from the Prince of Liechtenstein, 1954.

This tiny panel of the *Crucifixion*, with the Virgin Mary, St Mary Magdalen, and St John the Evangelist at the foot of the cross, was painted by an artist living in Catholic Antwerp at the time Luther was posting his theses in Wittenberg. Quentin Matsys, as we would expect from this devotional work, could not have been unconcerned with the controversy ending in the Reformation; indeed he was a friend and portraitist of one of the foremost Catholic figures, Erasmus, and known to at least one other, Thomas More. He was probably visited in Antwerp – for More suggests as much in a letter to Erasmus – by one of the contemporary painters most buffeted between the Catholic and Protestant worlds by the Reformation: Hans Holbein. And he certainly received in his home the artist for whom the Reformation was intellectually one of the most important events in his life – Albrecht Dürer.

When Quentin Matsys was painting this small panel Michelangelo had finished his heroic work on the Sistine Ceiling and Raphael was dead. Dürer, in visiting Antwerp (and Quentin) in 1520, was conscious of Raphael and mentioned him often in his diary. It is important to realize that in painting this *Crucifixion* Quentin was not being naive but, with at least a partial knowledge of what was being done in Italy, chose to employ the manner of earlier Flemish artists as a more appropriate way of expressing his religious feelings. He did this with particular subtlety in the colour, which ranges from the deep blue of the Virgin's robe to the violet of the Magdalen's to the warm orange-red of John's against the cool blue-green landscape. These colours make the event, which reaches its fullest meaning in the nails through Christ's feet and hands, more poignant. Perhaps most touching is the contrast between the figure of the Virgin, withdrawn into a deep blue cocoon in her sorrow, and John, with his luminous red hair bursting out against a redder garment in passionate and helpless protest. The forms of the landscape background seem to echo the anguish of the Crucifixion.

VII Bartel Beham

Nuremberg 1502 – Italy 1540

*Portrait of a Bavarian Prince, c.*1531

Oil on panel, 27½ x 22¾ in. (69.8 x 57.8 cm.)
No. 6187. Bought with Agnew as agent from the Prince of Liechtenstein, 1954.

The German artist, Bartel Beham, describes this effete young prince with the greatest subtlety. Although clad in fur, black brocade, and jewels, his body shrinks under their weight and his right hand clasps his left timorously. His skin is pink and cream, his features precise, and his hair a lustrous gold. Beham continues the analysis mercilessly by recording a timid display of jewellery for a sixteenth-century courtier, by flattening the black beret and dragging it down with a faintly lavender feather, even by threading the transparent white sleeves with stripes of gold. Finally Beham cruelly exposes this Bavarian prince against a background of stringent green.

This is a highly sophisticated work. The events of Bartel Beham's life might provide some clue to its very wordliness. He grew up in Nuremberg, which must have been dominated in the arts by the great figure of Albrecht Dürer, who was to die in 1527; certainly Beham's engravings and woodcuts show the influence, even if the younger man's Lucretias, Cleopatras, and children with death-heads show a morbidity more sensual and perhaps even more sensational than Dürer's intellectual explorations. The year Nuremberg became officially Lutheran – 1525 – Beham, a brother, and another painter-engraver were charged with disbelief in the Bible and Christ and in baptism and communion, and were expelled from Nuremberg for their heresies in religious and political matters. By 1527 Beham was in Munich and by 1530 he was court painter to one of its co-rulers, Duke Wilhelm IV of Bavaria. Ottawa's painting has always been considered the companion piece to a portrait Beham painted of Wilhelm's bachelor brother and ineffectual co-ruler, Ludwig. This is dated 1531 and is still in the Liechtenstein collection.

VIII Agnolo Bronzino

Monticelli 1503 — Florence 1572

Portrait of a Man, c.1540

Oil on panel, 42 x 32¾ in. (106.7 x 83.2 cm.)
No. 3717. Bought at Knoedler, London, 1930, on the advice of Charles Ricketts.

The attainments of the ideal Italian Renaissance courtier seem to be epitomized in this portrait of an unknown man by the Florentine painter Bronzino. One feels that both Niccolo Macchiavelli, whose *Il Principe* (*The Prince*) was published in 1513, and Baldassare Castiglione, whose *Il Cortegiano* (*The Courtier*) was published in 1528, would have admired the energy and self-possession with which he holds his body and dominates his clothes (unlike Beham's *Prince*, plate VII) while self-consciously affecting a relaxed gracefulness in his hands. They would have observed the exquisite grooming of even his bristling beard and appreciated the rich restraint of his clothes. They would have interpreted the presence of the cold blue statue of a *Venus Pudica* – symbol of a desirable erudition – as evidence of his interest both in the arts and in antiquity. Finally these virtues would have made them feel confident in this man's ability to command, which the self-assertion of his body, the calculating gaze of his eyes, and even the complete discipline of Bronzino's painting would reinforce. He could be a prince or a courtier. He was in fact as much their creation as Bronzino's.

A highly controlled painter in the Mannerist style, Bronzino was himself a generation younger than Castiglione and Machiavelli and worked in the period of the Renaissance appropriately called Mannerist. From the time of the marriage in 1539 of Cosimo I, Grand Duke of Tuscany, to Eleanor of Toledo, he was court painter and produced many such formal portraits of the Medici family. Although it is usually assumed that this work was painted after Bronzino became the Medici painter, the sitter has never been identified nor the work's date certainly established.

IX Hans Eworth

Holland ? — London 1574

*Portrait of Lady Dacre, c.*1558

Oil on panel, 29 x 22¾ in. (73.7 x 57.8 cm.)
No. 3337. Bought at Agnew, London, 1925, on the advice of Charles Ricketts.

The formidable woman in this portrait was born Mary Nevill, daughter of George Nevill, Lord Abergavenny, who had been a hunting companion of Henry VII and a favourite of Henry VIII. About 1537 she married Thomas Fiennes, ninth Baron Dacre, by whom she had three children. In the background of this picture hangs Dacre's portrait, painted, as is indicated on the frame, in 1540 when he was twenty-four – clearly long before this portrait of his wife. It is generally surmised that this is a lost portrait by Holbein. A year after it was painted Dacre was hanged, after a classic law case before the Lord Chancellor, for having been involved in the killing of a servant. If it were not that Lady Dacre went on to marry twice more, we could assume that she had commissioned the portrait from Eworth as a nostalgic record of dutiful widowhood. On the basis of the costume it is generally assumed that it was painted about 1555. The portrait may be a record of the restoration of family fortunes and titles in 1558.

Eworth was one of the many northern artists who made their way from the continent to England. He seems to have been born in Holland and is known to have worked in Antwerp in 1540 before arriving in England some six years after the death in 1543 of Hans Holbein, whose work must have influenced him.

By comparison with Holbein, Eworth is a vulgarian who found his perfect model in Lady Dacre. With posies tucked in at her neck, the embroidery of her collar and cuffs, the richly painted tapestry work behind the enshrined portrait of her late husband, her writing paraphernalia, it is hard to believe that she does not come from the nineteenth century. Even the recorded complaint of her daughter-in-law, Anne Sackville, that her husband Gregory was kept in undue subjection by his mother, has a modern ring. There is, however, a reminder in the severe and indomitable features of her face that she belonged to a sterner world and had been a subject of Henry VIII, Edward VI, and Mary and died in the reign of the first Elizabeth.

X Peter Paul Rubens

Siegen 1577 — Antwerp 1640

The Entombment of Christ, 1613–14

Oil on panel, 34¾ x 25¾ in. (88.3 x 65.4 cm.)
No. 6431. Bought with Agnew as agent from the Prince of Liechtenstein, 1956.

Two of the greatest artists of the Baroque meet in this small panel: Michelangelo Caravaggio, who had painted the original composition for this *Entombment* in 1604 for an altar in the church of Santa Maria Novicella (la Chiesa Nuova) in Rome, and Peter Paul Rubens, who finished the high altar for this same church in 1608. Rubens admired the older artist's work so much that he had that year persuaded his patron, the Duke of Mantua, to buy Caravaggio's *Death of the Virgin,* now in the Louvre. He remembered the *Entombment,* which he had seen daily, and painted this small, free version of it after he returned to Antwerp some time between 1613 and 1614.

Caravaggio's large altarpiece (now in the Vatican) is one of the monuments of early baroque art. Although the record clearly shows that Rubens liked the more brutal examples of Caravaggio's painting, he was himself a worldly man, a courtier, inclined to paint more colouristically, more sensuously, and more harmoniously.

Rubens made significant changes in Caravaggio's composition – most obviously in moving Mary Cleophas, whose arms are theatrically outstretched in the background of the other work. In keeping with a greater harmony of feeling, which he developed in all the figures, Rubens has the Madonna, with Mary Cleophas now beside her, look down with concern at the figure of Christ, and he has moved the red-clad St John further forward, with one foot on a step leading into the tomb as he compassionately supports the body of Christ. The whole is more cohesive and unified, the parts flow together in a more poignant realization of the physical facts of the weight of the body of Christ and of his death, than in the original *Entombment.* Rubens applied the paint with great fluidity and such assurance that, although certain parts – like the emphasized body of Christ – are solid paint, in other parts we see only the brown underpainting with which he worked out the basic composition and the forms. This free variation on a theme is a tribute to Caravaggio by another genius of the seventeenth century.

XI Orazio Gentileschi

Pisa 1563 – London 1639

Lot and his Daughters, 1621–6

Oil on canvas, 62 x 77 in. (157.5 x 195.6 cm.)
No. 14811. Bought with Agnew as agent at the Spencer-Churchill sale, Christie's, 1965.

Unlike earlier religious pictures in the National Gallery, this large baroque painting by Orazio Gentileschi was undoubtedly intended for a private collection rather than a religious institution. Its sensational subject is accurately biblical but not particularly appropriate for a church; on the other hand great private collectors became an important factor in the patronage of the artist in the seventeenth century. Orazio Gentileschi, in pursuit of such support, sold the original version of this subject to the Archbishop of Genoa before moving there from Rome in 1621, another to the Duke of Savoy before moving on to Turin, another to Marie de Médicis while considering a move to Paris, and yet another to Charles I of England. The version at Ottawa, which may be the boldest, was probably that of 1623 intended for the Duke of Savoy. After his stays in Genoa, Turin, and Paris, Orazio became court painter to Charles I in England, where he died.

The sensational implications of the story of incest in these paintings (Genesis XIX: 30–8) were part of the theatricality of the baroque that Orazio must have absorbed as it was flowering in Rome, where he went as a boy and lived until 1621. Orazio had known Caravaggio and an important Bolognese follower of Caravaggio, Guido Reni, and was influenced by both artists in the boldness of his subject and the drama of its rendering. His handling of forms is larger and more decorative than Caravaggio's; the decorative quality increased by the clarity of the colours – the rose, the greyed blue, the gold and white of the garments against the pale flesh and the dark of the cave. He retained Caravaggio's dramatic gestures, particularly in the attitude of one of Lot's daughters, who points histrionically toward the rolling fields of the landscape at the right. In some versions she points to a burning Sodom, but this landscape is intended to be the paradise Lot and his daughters had lost. The work, therefore, is presumably an allegory of original sin.

XII Rembrandt van Rijn

Leyden 1606 – Amsterdam 1669

*The Toilet of Esther, c.*1633

Oil on canvas, 43 x 37 in. (109.2 x 94 cm.)
No. 6089. Bought with Schab as agent from the Prince of Liechtenstein, 1953.

The last digit of the date on this work is almost impossible to decipher and has been read as a 2, a 3, a 4 and a 7; in any case it must have been painted after Rembrandt moved from Leyden to Amsterdam in 1631. There is a similar confusion about the subject, which has been called *The Jewish Bride, The Toilet of Bathsheba*, and *The Toilet of Esther.* Modern scholars prefer Esther, whose deliverance of the Jews seventeenth-century Holland equated with its own deliverance from Catholic Spain.

If this is Esther, the painting illustrates part of a single sentence in the *Book of Esther*: 'Now it came to pass on the third day, that Esther put on her royal apparel . . .'. The three days had been days of fasting and prayer before going to Ahasuerus (or Xerxes), her husband and king, to declare herself a Jew and to ask that the order to destroy all the Jews of Xerxes' great kingdom, which stretched even into India, be revoked. (The Jews celebrate the consequent deliverance in the Feast of Purim.) If this is indeed the subject of this painting, it would explain its seriousness. The young woman's solemnity, even her radiant paleness, are consistent with the story. Her hair, which the blue-clad maidservant combs so reverently, is as soft and fair as Esther's should be. And certainly her garments are royal – her skirt woven of shining metal threads, her gossamer-like white sleeves embroidered with blue and gold, her tunic the richest of soft red velvet, its border heavily encrusted with gold and, at the neck, with gems. It is typical of Rembrandt that, even though he was still a young man in his twenties and capable of such bravura with colour and paint, he could restrain these effects by enveloping them in the total play of light and shadow and by neutralizing them in the very dullness of the background; consequently the gravity of the young woman we assume to be Esther is radiant.

XIII Jacob Jordaens

Antwerp 1593–1678

'As the Old Sing, So the Young Twitter', c.1640

Oil on canvas, 57¼ x 85¾ in. (145.5 x 218 cm.)
No. 15790. Bought with Agnew as agent at auction Sotheby's, London, from the Earl of Wemyss and March, 1969.

Few paintings embrace us as immediately in a spirit of revelry and self-indulgence as this large canvas. It invites our fingers to stroke flesh, wicker, brass, pewter, gold, pottery, glass; our palate to taste grapes, wine, shrimp, chicken, lemon, herring, and beer; our ears to listen to human song, two flutes and the piping of one young bird; and even our mouth, like the infant's, to be pacified by its horn. And our eyes are constantly tantalized and pleased by what they can find – a dog, an owl, a candlestick. The whole is painted with great variety and confidence by Jordaens, who had worked with Rubens and van Dyck and, with their deaths, was soon to become the senior painter of Antwerp.

This, however, is something more than a painting to tantalize our senses. Its meaning does not seem to be clarified by the poem (by the contemporary Dutch Calvinist poet Jacob Cats), whose title Jordaens borrowed for at least four paintings, one tapestry, and one engraving on this theme. It was usually paired as a subject with *The King Drinks*, clearly a Twelfth Night painting, which would also explain this revelry. In the upper left-hand corner there is an exquisite piece of still life in which the perishable flowers and the snuffed candle (which in another version are combined with a skull) were considered reminders of death, a *memento mori* in the midst of the jollity. This could be a conventional expression of seriousness, but there is also in the old woman's hand a piece of paper that begins with a reference to a Spanish victory near Antwerp in 1638 and goes on to 'Die Geusen' or The Beggars, the first words of a rousing song about those who, since 1566, had resisted Spanish rule in the Low Countries. Since Jordaens eventually became Protestant the work may be an early expression of his skepticism about both the political and religious freedom of Flanders under Catholic Spain. It may be significant, but at the moment by no means clarifying, that Jordaens introduced his own portrait as the jester holding the cage with the three small birds. Perhaps the painting is an allegory on the foolishness of mindless enjoyment in captivity.

XIV Bartolomé Esteban Murillo

Seville 1618–1682

Abraham and the Three Angels, 1670–4

Oil on canvas, 93 x 103 in. (236.2 x 261.6 cm.)
No. 4900. Bought at Agnew, London, 1948.

For the chapel of the hospital of La Caridad in his native Seville, Murillo painted six large canvases to be placed very high above the altar on the walls of the chapel; two of them are still to be seen in their original location. Of the four paintings that were removed from the chapel by the Napoleonic general, Marshal Soult, two were later sold to the Duke of Sutherland – one of them Ottawa's; the other, its companion, the *Return of the Prodigal Son* that is now in Washington.

Since the purposes of La Caridad were charitable, Murillo, who since 1665 had been a member of the lay order that supported it, based his subjects on acts of good works in the Old and New Testaments. Therefore in *Abraham and the Three Angels* the emphasis is not upon the annunciation to Sarah of the birth of Isaac but on Abraham falling to the ground before three strangers and offering them, with eloquent gestures, water to wash, and rest, and food. Beside this work hung the *Prodigal Son.*

Murillo seems to have spent the whole of his virtuous life in his native Seville, where he was so highly regarded as a painter that he was made a member of the charitable order of La Caridad itself. He painted pictures of extraordinary innocence. The three angels here are concerned but untroubled as they stand in garments of limpid blue and pink and violet, with sashes of gold and peacock and vermilion. Abraham is noble as he offers everything he possesses. Even the landscape, although very light and painted freely since it was intended to be seen from a distance, is open and idyllic. Murillo justified his fame in Seville by adapting with great skill the composition and the painting of this work to its ultimate location high in the chapel. He even related the movement of the feet of the angels to Abraham's leg so that they could be seen from below as if they were part of a stately dance. With a sense of drama common to the century in which he lived, Murillo carried this subdued movement through the arms and staffs of the angels to the strong and persuasive gestures of the kneeling Abraham.

XV Hyacinthe Rigaud

Perpignan 1659 – Paris 1743

The Le Juge Family, 1699

Oil on canvas, 45 x 58 in. (114.3 x 147.3 cm.)
No. 4310. Bought with Colnaghi as agent at auction Sotheby's, London, 1938.

Rigaud was a successful and circumspect painter whose patronage came from the court of Louis XIV at Versailles. This large painting of Jean Le Juge, his wife Elisabeth, and their daughter Marguerite-Charlotte, was an important personal document for Rigaud because eight years after dating it 1699 he married Elisabeth Le Juge, then widowed three years. The marriage seems to have been an extraordinarily happy one. When Rigaud painted his self-portrait some time after 1729 for his native town of Perpignan he included in the background the outlines of his wife and her daughter from Ottawa's painting, a testimony of its significance for him.

The portrait has a baroque splendour. The figures are majestic, the materials colourful and shining; the brown curtain is pulled over the severe architecture of the rotunda in a device of the period. The three members of the Le Juge family behave with a dignity that would have been appropriate at Versailles. At the same time we are reminded of the fact that it was painted on the very eve of the eighteenth century by the animation in the features of the mother and child, by the parakeet teasing the dog, and by the prettiness of the flowers, which were probably painted by another artist.

XVI Jean-Baptiste-Siméon Chardin

Paris 1699–1779

The Nursemaid, 1738

Oil on canvas, 18⅜ x 14¾ in. (46.7 x 37.5 cm.)
No. 6432. Bought with Agnew as agent from the Prince of Liechtenstein, 1956.

If we consider *The Nursemaid* in the light of *The Le Juge Family* by Rigaud (plate XV), we realize how unassertive Chardin was. First of all the canvas is about one-tenth the size of the Rigaud. The colours are quieter, the materials in the painting gentler and humbler, the figures modestly set back in space. But this apparently unpretentious work is a painting of the highest visual sensibility, designed to flatter the eyes of the connoisseur who could take it in his hands and appreciate Chardin's understatement.

The subject is charming: a nursemaid leans over to a valiant little boy who is about to go through the open door with a book under his arm, leaving on the floor behind him his cards and his battledore and shuttlecock. Theoretically the emphasis should be upon the nursemaid who sits on a pinkish-red chair, the warmest colour in the room, which is reflected in the wall behind her and caught up in one ball of wool, the cards, and more palely in the flesh. Her dress is a combination of blues painted more energetically than anything else in the work, her apron and cap a rough white with the thickest loading of paint; in her left hand the boy's black tricorne hat makes the strongest contrast in values. But it is the figure of the boy that is most significant. Standing quietly in front of the door that opens into a corridor with a blued wall; dressed in a grey that, like his skin, has picked up the pink of the chair; his collar and buttons echoing the nursemaid's white; his hair tied with a ribbon of her blue, which also runs as a line down his neckline and cuff – the boy provides the quiet resolution of all the colours in the room and finally dominates it.

It was in the Salon of 1739 that, along with five other domestic genre scenes, Chardin exhibited this version of *The Nursemaid*, the only one to survive. Among the other five scenes was another version of Ottawa's *La Pourvoyeuse* (plate 41), which a Prince of Liechtenstein bought with *The Nursemaid* when he was Ambassador to Paris between 1737 and 1741.

XVII Benjamin West

Springfield, Pennsylvania 1738 – London 1820

The Death of Wolfe, 1770

Oil on canvas, 59½ x 84 in. (151.1 x 213.4 cm.)
No. 8007. Gift of the Duke of Westminster, 1918.

Probably the most famous work in Ottawa's collection is Benjamin West's *Death of Wolfe*, which the Duke of Westminster, a descendant of its first owner, gave through Lord Beaverbrook as a tribute to Canada's role in the First World War.

Several legends have grown up around this painting. One is that it is historically accurate. In fact it is a highly fantasized account of the death of the commander of the victorious British forces on the Plains of Abraham by a painter who had never been to Québec. (Only one figure, the young officer above Wolfe holding the flag – Lt. Henry Brown – could have been with Wolfe at that moment.) From 1759, the year of the battle, until 1770, the year West dated this work, there had been time to romanticize this event by which the British asserted their supremacy in Canada. There is also a legend about West's radicalism in his insistence upon historical veracity in the use of contemporary costumes, which we are often told – quite inaccurately – he was the first to employ in painting such a current event.

The *Death of Wolfe* is a great neoclassic painting in which the unities of time and space are ignored as irrelevant. Around the figure of Wolfe, which is based upon numerous *Entombments* of Christ, there is a frieze of figures symbolizing the Americas, derived from various other works of art. These allusions, along with the bold colours, the scale of the large work, even the smoke of battle in the background over the St Lawrence, have a certain grandeur and memorability that can explain its reputation.

It immediately became famous. A Pennsylvania Quaker, West went to live in England after spending three critical years (1760 to 1763) in Rome, where he absorbed the neoclassicism of Mengs, Battoni, and Gavin Hamilton. He exhibited this at the Royal Academy in 1771 and then sold it to Lord Grosvenor. He was commissioned to paint three other versions, including one for George III, and is reputed to have made £5,000 from the sale of engravings after the work.

XVIII William von Moll Berczy

Wallvenstein, Swabia 1774 — New York 1813

The Woolsey Family, 1809

Oil on canvas, 23¾ x 34¼ in. (60.3 x 87 cm.)
No. 5875. Gift of Major Edward C. Woolsey, 1952.

The Woolsey Family was painted half a century after West's *The Death of Wolfe* (plate XVII) by an artist who, unlike West, knew the ramparts of Québec. He painted them here – seen through a window – in a room with people who represented a certain reconciliation between the English (or at least the Irish) and the French. The young man standing is John William Woolsey, a merchant, soldier, and banker who had been born forty-one years before in Québec, the son of a Protestant Irishman and of the woman we see to his right, the former Joséphette Rottot. Her sympathetically painted daughter-in-law was born Julie Lemoine. Julie's brother, Benjamin Lemoine, sits with his flute by the window. The painting was given to the National Gallery by Major Edward C. Woolsey, who described himself as the great-grandson of one of the four boys, the baby held in his mother's lap.

The painter was an émigré who, by the time he arrived near Toronto in 1794 after a series of misadventures, considered himself a Canadian. Born Johann Albrecht Ulrich Moll in Bavaria, he was educated at Leipzig and Jena Universities. He married in Switzerland in 1785, using the alias Guillaume Berczy, and then went to Italy for five years before moving in 1790 to London. In 1792 he accompanied a group of German settlers to the United States. When he ran into difficulties there, he moved on to Canada where he finally found that painting provided his only satisfactory livelihood.

Although a member of the Woolsey family was later to glue a piece of paper to the back of this canvas describing the artist as an 'amateur' – it is true that he was in the tradition of the itinerant New England limner, painting each figure for ten pounds and adding the dog free – Berczy did reveal the worldliness of his European background in his adjustment of the scene to the contemporary neoclassic mode. He organized the figures as if they formed a frieze, restrained the dignified interior so that it is enriched only by a few classical mouldings and details, and gave stylized, classicizing costumes to the group at the right.

XIX J. M. W. Turner

London 1775–1851

Mercury and Argus, 1836

Oil on canvas, 59 x 43 in. (149.9 x 109.2 cm.)
No. 5795. Bought from Agnew, London, 1951.

Turner, the English Romantic, had reached the peak of his powers when he painted *Mercury and Argus* and exhibited it at the Royal Academy in 1836, three years before the more famous *Fighting Téméraire.* Although his chief propagandist, John Ruskin, argued that even *Mercury and Argus* was an example of Turner's 'scientific or essentially truthful system', we are today less impressed by the geological and botanical knowledge, which may exist under the structure of this landscape, than by the sheer fantasy expressed in seemingly translucent glazes of coloured paint.

There is every evidence that Turner's landscapes derived from the seventeenth-century French painter Claude, but his countryside is wilder, the towns surmount hills more mysteriously, trees bend more perilously, tumultuous water and land are more difficult to separate. The sources for his motives are richer than Claude's for, in addition to the Temple of the Sibyls at Tivoli rising at the right, he used other forms derived from his travels down the Rhine and from the Scottish coast. Intoxicated by his first visit to Venice and by Venetian painting, his light became more colourful, more intense and more pervasive than anything in Claude.

Turner's subjects often deal with disaster – the burning of the Houses of Parliament or the sinking of ships at sea. *Mercury and Argus* also deals with the possibilities of both death and escape – death for hundred-eyed Argus, whom Mercury is charming to sleep with a tune on his reeds so that he may sever his head and 'send it bloody and rolling over the rocks'; escape for the white heifer, in reality Io, whom the yellow light picks out below Mercury and Argus and who was 'white and shining, lovely even in altered form'. In spite of Ruskin's objection to the use of the word 'sublime' and particularly to the interpretation of it by Edmund Burke in his *On the Sublime and the Beautiful,* published in 1756, this painting in its subject, its cavernous depths and radiant sky, in its very obscurity, is an ideal argument for Burke's explanation of sublimity.

XX Antoine Plamondon

Ancienne-Lorette 1804 – Neuville 1895

Portrait of Sister Saint-Alphonse, 1841

Oil on canvas, 36 x 28½ in. (91.4 x 72.4 cm.)
No. 4297. Purchased from Mrs Antoine Schwartz, Québec, 1937.

About 1840 Antoine Plamondon painted portraits of nuns in the Hôpital-Général, Québec. This portrait of Sister Saint-Alphonse was commissioned by her father and remained with the family until it was acquired by the National Gallery. She was born Marie-Emilie Pelletier, the daughter of a prosperous merchant and of a fashionable woman Plamondon had painted a decade before.

Plamondon, who was born near Québec, studied from 1819 to 1825 with the Québec-born, self-taught, and highly expressive artist Joseph Légaré; during this time he helped his teacher restore some paintings that an émigré priest had brought from France. In 1826, when he was still only twenty-two, he was given the money to study in Paris, where he remained as a pupil of Paulin Guérin, a follower of David, until the Revolution of 1830 in which his sympathies were with the losing Louis-Philippe. He then returned to Québec.

The French experience helps explain the increased serenity and solidity of Plamondon's works. He must have known paintings of nuns by French artists like Philippe de Champaigne and Largillière, with their consciousness of the decorative possibilities of convent dress. His own quietly pious description of Sister Saint-Alphonse's face is appealing; she is obviously much younger and more responsive than his *Mother Saint-Anne,* commissioned for the Hôpital-Général about the same time. Enlivened by the silver cross and the red prayer book and chair, the white and black of her habit obviously gave Plamondon great pleasure, particularly as he contained the softly painted sleeves and cloak within the austerity of the total design. Behind the nun he painted a light that seems to glow from her saintly presence.

Although Plamondon, an irascible man, retired to the country and gave up painting on commission in 1851, he did become one of the founding members of the Royal Canadian Academy in 1880; his diploma work was Ottawa's *Still Life* (plate XXV).

XXI Honoré Daumier

Marseilles 1808 – Valmondois 1879

Third-Class Carriage

Oil on canvas, 26¾ x 36⅝ in. (67 x 93 cm.)
No. 4633. Bought 1946 from G. C. Edwards, Ottawa.

Ottawa has the most finished, and probably the final, version of one of the most memorable images produced by a nineteenth-century painter, the *Third-Class Carriage* of Honoré Daumier. The more famous version is the unfinished canvas in the Metropolitan Museum in New York in which the figures are more strongly caricatured and the nervously penetrating line is more apparent. Ottawa's is gentler – sympathetic rather than polemical.

The figures huddled together in any of the versions of the *Third-Class Carriage* represent Daumier's concern for the working people of France. He expressed this wittily and with great visual brilliance in the thousands of lithographic cartoons he had produced for the daily newspapers *La Caricature* and *Le Charivari*. In his later years he turned to painting as a more compassionate means of conveying the nature of their lives. But the caricaturist's eye and hand were still at work, seizing the most revealing feature and gesture but generalizing them, so that each figure becomes the symbol of a social state rather than of an individual human being.

Daumier was absorbed in the problem of the world's dispossessed – of the Don Quixotes, the mountebanks, the fugitives who wandered over the face of the earth. Nineteenth-century transportation and, in particular, the railroad train provided a means of placing travellers in a limbo between the point of departure and their destination. Here in the smoky third-class carriage, in which the colours seem to contain the struggle of light against particles of smoke, the young mother nursing her child, the parchment-skinned old woman, and the sleeping boy, arouse our protective instincts.

This painting was in the famous exhibition of Daumier's work at Durand-Ruel in Paris in 1878. A watercolour study for it exists in the Walters Art Gallery, Baltimore.

XXII Lucius R. O'Brien

Shanty Bay 1832 — Toronto 1899

Sunrise on the Saguenay, 1880

Oil on canvas, $34\frac{1}{2}$ x $49\frac{1}{2}$ in. (87.6 x 125.7 cm.)
No. 113. R.C.A. diploma work 1880.

When the first exhibition of the Royal Canadian Academy of Art was held in 1880 and the Academicians deposited their works for 'The National Gallery of Art', which had no other existence, Lucius O'Brien was the Academy's first president and gave as his diploma work this *Sunrise on the Saguenay*, which he had dated that year. It must, therefore, have been one of the first works in the Gallery's collection. (The first patron of the Royal Canadian Academy, the Marquis of Lorne, saw to it that his mother-in-law, Queen Victoria, bought three paintings by O'Brien that year for the royal collection.)

Lucius O'Brien was born in Upper Canada (now Ontario), in a town on Lake Simcoe that his father, an English lieutenant-colonel, had helped found and that had the unprepossessing name of Shanty Bay. He was educated at Toronto's Upper Canada College, the Canadian equivalent of an English public school, was articled to an architect, and then worked as a surveyor throughout Canada. As a surveyor he followed an established Canadian tradition in making topographical drawings and watercolours. It was 1870 before he decided to become a painter.

O'Brien was conscious of contemporary American painting – of the work of George Caleb Bingham (1811–79) of St Louis, of the English-born Thomas Moran (1837–1926), and in particular of Albert Bierstadt (1830–1902), who actually came to Canada when Lord Dufferin and Lord Lorne were Governors-General. Like these Americans, and unlike the Impressionists working at the same time in France, O'Brien felt a romantic attraction to spectacular forms of nature such as the great treeless cliffs of the Saguenay River, which flows into the St Lawrence about 120 miles north-east of Québec. His light is also American – even and translucent. He did not hesitate to paint his sunrise in pink and green or to pick out the plants on the shore with the freest strokes of paint. The result is a landscape of tranquil grandeur.

XXIII Edgar Degas

Paris 1834–1917

*Woman with an Umbrella, c.*1886–7

Oil on canvas, 24 x 19¾ in. (61 x 50.2 cm.)
No. 15838. Bought from Feilchenfeldt, Zurich, 1969.

When Sigmund Freud was studying with Charcot in Paris in 1885–6, he wrote to Vienna: 'The ugliness of Paris women can hardly be exaggerated: not a decent pretty face.' It was about that time and in that place that Edgar Degas painted this woman, who was in all probability a dancer. With a dancer's discipline she holds herself back; her umbrella is ready for attack, her head held high above the neckpiece of grey fur. Her clothes have a certain elegant restraint, but this does not distract our attention from that compelling – and ugly – face.

If we think for a moment of the sugary prettiness of female portraits painted by the artists of the contemporary Salon, we can see how such ugliness could have been an act of faith on the part of an artist who, at the time of the first Impressionist exhibition, had described himself as a realist. His realism is something more subtle, however, than the choice of a homely model. Degas makes us see this woman's tensions, her defences, even a slight self-mockery – in short her complexity – with a penetration even Freud might have respected.

Behind the restraint and distinction of this painting is Degas's admiration for, and analysis of, the work of great portraitists of the past, in particular Holbein, Ingres, and Delacroix. Having made copies of such works as a self-portrait drawing by Filippino Lippi in the Uffizi and of an oil sketch by Memling in the Louvre, he understood the expressive possibilities of a painting that might seem unfinished. It is true here that the very sketchiness of the painting – the brusque strokes of paint in some areas against the smoothness of the skin – and the very mobility of the face, with the nose and mouth twisted, one eye shadowed, the brows raised, give us the feeling that this woman is emerging before us.

Finally the sitter, prickly and defensive though she might have been, possesses the quality Degas admired most: will. It explains her proud pose, her distinguished dress, even the mobility of that harsh face. It is what makes her, as the French would say, 'une jolie laide'.

XXIV Vincent van Gogh

Zundert, Holland 1853 — Auvers 1890

Iris, 1889

Oil on paper laid on canvas, 24½ x 19 in. (62.2 x 48.3 cm.)
No. 6294. Bought from van Wisselingh, Amsterdam, 1955.

In May 1889 the Dutch painter Vincent van Gogh, who had been in France since 1886, went into an asylum at St Rémy as a voluntary patient. At first he was content to paint within the garden of the asylum. As he wrote to Theo: 'Since I have been here, the deserted garden, planted with large pines beneath which the grass grows tall and unkempt and mixed with various weeds, has sufficed for my work.' The requests to Theo for canvas were made so frequently that it seems likely he exhausted his supply, for this work is on paper that has been applied to canvas since. It is nevertheless painted so freely and with such liberal strokes of paint that Vincent must have felt he was working on a stronger support.

Perhaps the sense of protection given him by the cloistered garden at St Rémy made Vincent ready to approach a humble plant (quite different from his dramatic paintings of sunflowers the year before). As he wrote to his sister Willemien in October 1889: 'I often paint things like that – as insignificant and as dramatic as a dusty blade of grass by the roadside.' In this painting the tall and unkempt grasses, mixed with weeds, as he had described them to Theo, form a radiant background for the irises. He must have painted the grass and weeds rapidly but with considerable calculation for they are all in a rhythmic relationship to one another as if they were radiating from a single source – the bulb of the iris plant. Against their vibrancy the iris stands out principally because the strokes for its leaves are bolder and more continuous; its flowers are only discovered faintly emerging in their blue from the pink, yellow, and green background. The only flower in full bloom is sensually soft in form and colour.

It is possible that Vincent always intended this work for Willemien, who was to own it, for in consoling her that year for what seems to have been an unhappy love affair he philosophized in his letters to her and once, in comparing human beings to wheat, wrote: 'Aren't we forced to submit to growing like a plant without the power to move?'

XXV Ozias Leduc

Saint-Hilaire 1864 — Saint-Hyacinthe 1955

Still Life — Study by the Light of a Candle, 1893

Oil on canvas, 14 x 18 in. (35.6 x 45.7 cm.)
No. 6402. Bought from the Dominion Gallery, Montreal, 1955.

Vincent van Gogh would have envied Ozias Leduc — living in the small Québec village of St Hilaire where he had been born; painting religious works for a livelihood and small still-life or genre paintings for his own pleasure; uncontaminated by too much knowledge of art or the world; with a natural skill in spite of the fact that he, like Van Gogh, was essentially self-taught. Van Gogh would even have romanticized his piety and his later interest in the theories of Maurice Denis about art and religion.

When Ozias Leduc painted this still life he had not as yet made his one trip to France with another Québec painter, Suzor-Côté; that was to be in 1897. His work was therefore remarkably unaffected. It nevertheless participated in the Symbolist movement that was spreading throughout the world, for Leduc used his candle almost ritualistically to light the homely objects he had assembled and painted as if there was virtue in their simplicity. The radiance of the candle's light in the darkness inevitably suggests the work of the French seventeenth-century painter Georges de la Tour, which Leduc may have known from reproductions. The painting's brownness may have been the result of his having seen old pictures covered with dirty varnish and considering this the colour for the art of museums. (He did exhibit it the year it was painted in the spring show of the first art museum in Canada, the Art Association of Montreal.) The result is a small still life that has great dignity and a certain spiritual force.

XXVI Gustav Klimt

Baumgarten 1862 — Vienna 1918

Hope I, 1903

Oil on canvas, 71 x 26 in. (180.3 x 66 cm.)
No. 16579. Bought from Arte Moderna, Turin, 1970.

Whereas the symbolism of Ozias Leduc working in a Québec village was unassuming (plate XXV), the symbolism of Gustav Klimt painting this figure of *Hope* in Vienna in 1903 was full of pretensions. Klimt knew contemporary painting and deliberately followed Symbolism and Art Nouveau; in fact he was the energetic figure behind the Austrian branch of the movement, the Wiener Sezession, founded in 1897. In somewhat eclectic fashion *Hope* can sum up most of the character of the Symbolist movement throughout Europe.

First of all it is joyously derivative. From Anglo-Saxon times comes the ornament on the right, from Jan van Eyck's Eve on the Ghent altarpiece the inspiration for a pregnant nude, and from recent Pointillism in France the luminous handling of the flesh. The grotesque heads and skull in the background could have been drawn from the work of two other artists in the movement – the Norwegian Edvard Munch and the Belgian James Ensor. The stylized pattern and sinuous contours are part of the vocabulary of Art Nouveau as they are found, for example, in the drawing of Aubrey Beardsley. Literary allusions are common in works in this style, and such a source is not unlikely for the black monster at the left.

The painting is not a wholesome record of pregnancy, nudity, and hope. That such a scrawny, adolescent body should be pregnant and nude, its face gaunt but nevertheless surrounded with generous golden hair sprinkled with delicate blue forget-me-nots, seems perverse, and Klimt placed this unlikely symbol of hope against a background of artificially fabricated dreams and haunting nightmares, including the prospect of death. The skepticism, the irony, the expression of fears in such a decorative form are very much part of a movement that embraced Oscar Wilde, Huysmans, and D'Annunzio in literature.

XXVII David Milne

Bruce County 1882 — Toronto 1953

Billboards, 1912

Oil on canvas, 20 x 22⅛ in. (50.8 x 56.2 cm.)
No. 9850. Gift of the Picture Loan Society, 1962.

Billboards is an early work by David Milne, who throughout his life painted with great consistency. His works are unpretentious – small and spontaneous – but they play demandingly and animatedly with the eyes of the beholder. This is a simple street scene of the early twentieth century, but Milne has applied the colours and the paint deftly and sparingly to suggest animation and gaiety.

After having grown up on an Ontario farm and having taught in a country school, Milne went to New York in 1904 to study at the Art Students' League. He remained there, working as a commercial artist, visiting Stieglitz's Photo-Secession Gallery regularly, and exhibiting (as the lone Canadian) in the Armory Show of 1913, a year after *Billboards* was painted. (It is tempting to think that *Billboards* was the work then called *Columbus Circle* and exhibited as no. 796.) From 1915 he lived alternatively in the New England or New York countryside, except for a period in the Canadian Army during the war, and returned to live in Ontario permanently in 1928. Again he chose to live in the country rather than in Toronto.

This painting is important to the National Gallery not only as an early Milne but also as the gift of the Picture Loan Society of Toronto, which was organized and subsidized by the late Douglas Duncan, a close friend and supporter of Milne. A large part of Duncan's collection of Milnes was given from his estate to the National Gallery.

XXVIII Tom Thomson

Claremont, Ontario 1877 – Canoe Lake 1917

The Jack Pine, 1916–17

Oil on canvas, 50½ x 55 in. (127.6 x 139.7 cm.)
No. 1519. Bought from artist's estate, 1918.

The Symbolist movement became so pervasive that it influenced the architecture, the furnishings, the commercial art of the time. As a result Tom Thomson, an Ontario painter who never travelled in Europe and who had no formal academic training as an artist, could absorb it almost unconsciously as a way of thinking and painting.

Jack Pine would have been painted in the small shack where Thomson lived and worked near the Studio Building in a Toronto ravine, but it was based on sketches made at Lake Cauchon in Algonquin Park where Thomson had gone for the first time in 1912 and where he died in 1917 in what was officially described as a canoeing accident (it has, however, since been speculated that he was murdered or committed suicide). This artist worked as a commercial designer in Seattle from 1901 to 1905 and in a Toronto firm of engravers with other artists who, after his death, were to form the Group of Seven. But he was happiest in the Canadian wilds and we are told that he was a superb canoeist and woodsman. It is curious, therefore, that his landscapes are so uninhabited and so uninhabitable; there is never a foothold for human enjoyment. They are rarely painted in full summer. His trees have the bare branches of spring or fall, or of burned-out land, or they are burdened with snow in the winter. If there is not a storm, there is usually a sunrise or sunset. It is not too much to assume a symbolic intention behind such choices.

Thomson's brushstrokes were sure and calligraphic as he described the wet snow on the deep blue Lake Cauchon islands or brushed heavy horizontal strokes of paint across the canvas for the orange and green sky and the duller green-blue water. But against the dying light and sky the scraggly forms of the *Jack Pine* are most dramatic, its branches struggling to life but dominated by dark-green, tattered, bat-like forms as if the tree were a symbol – beautiful, oriental, but a symbol nevertheless of Thomson's wish for his own death on this spot.

Jack Pine was acquired the year after Thomson's death through Thomson's chief supporter, the late Dr J. M. MacCallum.

XXIX Fernand Léger

Argentan 1881 – Gife-sur-Yvette 1955

The Mechanic, 1920

Oil on canvas, $45\frac{1}{2}$ x $34\frac{3}{4}$ in. (116 x 89 cm.)
No. 14985. Bought from Louis Carré, Paris, 1966.

Ottawa's collection can demonstrate the effects of Cubism rather than the rarified forms of analytical Cubism itself. One of these effects was Fernand Léger's simplification of subtle, indefinite, mobile Cubist forms into bold geometric shapes of primary colours; these were used to present the mechanized world of the twentieth century. In the background of *The Mechanic* we can see how such forms produce a brash, extroverted rhythm with none of the mysteries of the analytical Cubist relationship of forms. Against this background stands the independent artisan of the twentieth century – the mechanic with a body that is proudly muscular, as efficient as a machine. He gives his body the same care he would give a mechanical object, shaping his moustache confidently, polishing his hair, decorating his arm with a tattoo and one of his fingers with two rings. In every sense he belongs to the twentieth century and represents a social revolution that gave him his proud independence. It is not surprising that Léger's political sympathies were communist.

Léger, the son of a Norman farmer who had fought and been gassed in the First World War, had just reached his most decisive personal vision of the world about the time he painted *The Mechanic.* It was the year before, for example, that he painted his large and characteristic canvas, *The City,* which is now in the Philadelphia Museum of Art; it was four years afterwards that he produced the significant film, *Le Ballet mécanique*; and it was in the same year, 1920, that he met the architect Le Corbusier.

During the Second World War Léger spent five years in America – teaching at Yale and in California but largely living in New York, a city that might have seemed his own creation. He also visited Québec and Montreal – one of the few great European artists of the twentieth century to do so.

XXX Piet Mondrian

Amersfoort, Utrecht 1872 – New York 1944

Composition with Blue Square, 1936–42

Oil on canvas, 24$\frac{7}{16}$ x 23$\frac{3}{4}$ in. (62.1 x 60.3 cm.)
No. 15911. Bought from Museum of Modern Art, New York, 1970.

Mondrian was a Dutch artist whose work, like Léger's, developed from analytical Cubism but toward an even greater simplification of forms and toward an even stronger conviction about the necessity of using only clean primary colours. But Mondrian's interests were not social and tangible, unlike Léger's; his reduction of painting to rectangles of primary colour was intended to suggest certain abstract concepts – ideals toward which man should order his life. He wrote that it was thanks to art that 'the laws of balance can be directly visualized'. Although decidedly Dutch and intimately involved with the Dutch movement De Stijl, which came into existence in 1917, Mondrian developed as an artist in Paris where he lived from 1912 to 1914 and to which he returned in 1919; during the Paris years between 1919 and 1938 he produced his most serenely balanced works.

It was in Paris that Mondrian began the *Composition with Blue Square,* but he probably took it with him to London for the two years he spent there from 1938, and finally in 1940 to New York where he finished it. With characteristic neatness he recorded the years 36/42 on the black line to the right of the blue square.

Nothing could be more pristine than the colour of this work – only black and white punctuated by one blue square. But although balance is its basic ingredient, the distribution of the lines, which are largely unbroken and continuous, is animated, even nervous. Where they intersect there is an optical illusion of a certain radiance. This greater vitality in the tension of the lines could be explained by its completion in New York, a city Mondrian loved and that was to inspire his most animated paintings, like *New York City* and *Broadway Boogie-Woogie.*

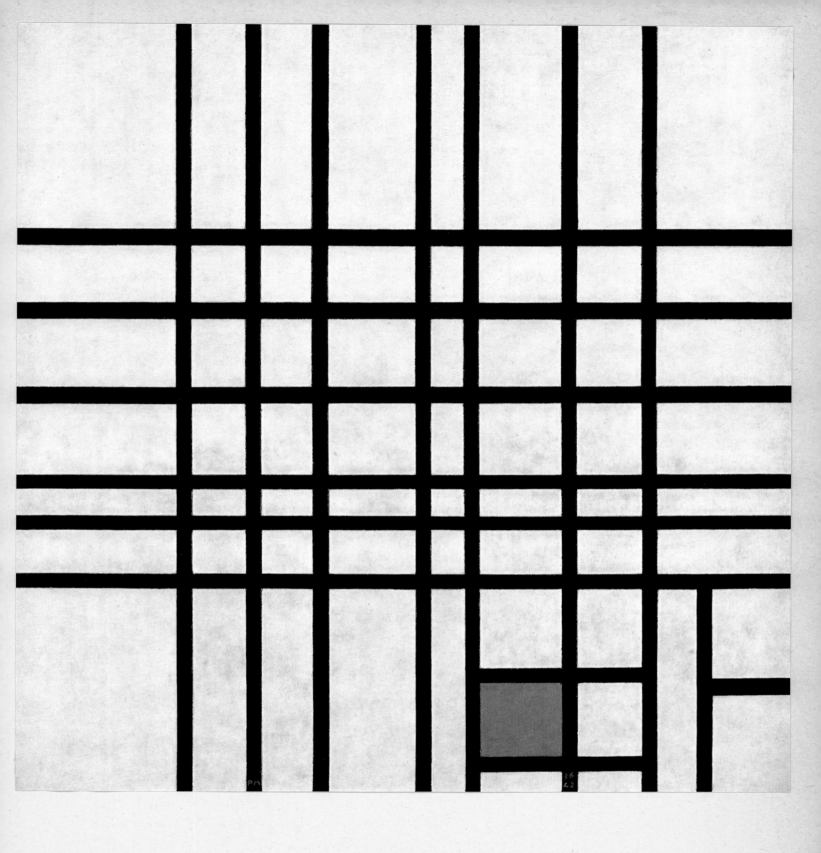

XXXI Jackson Pollock

Cody, Wyoming 1912 – East Hampton 1956

No. 29, 1950

Oil and other materials on glass, 48 x 72 in. (121.9 x 182.9 cm.)
No. 15462. Bought from the artist's widow, 1967.

In the mid-twentieth century there were two forms of abstraction – one, like Mondrian's and Léger's, growing out of Cubism and essentially concrete and happily contained within a finite frame, and the other perhaps reaching its ultimate expression in the work of Jackson Pollock. This second form developed from the organic and lyrical abstractions of the Russian Kandinsky and tried to free itself from any sense of a physical, finite order. Indeed in the year Pollock painted Ottawa's *No. 29, 1950*, he said in an interview that 'There was a reviewer a while back who wrote that my pictures didn't have any beginnings or any end. He didn't mean it as a compliment, but it was.' This form of abstraction was stimulated by the emphasis of the Surrealists on the unconscious. When, during the war, Pollock was asked about the advantages of having so many European artists in America, he didn't mention Mondrian or Léger but said, thinking of the Surrealists: 'I am particularly impressed with their concept of the source of art being the unconscious.'

In possessing Pollock's only work on glass, along with a print of Hans Namuth's film of Pollock painting it, Ottawa may have one of the most important documents in the movement that is called, in spite of Pollock's dislike of the term, Abstract Expressionism. On the glass itself we can see the result of the gestures by which Pollock spontaneously and without preliminary studies produced the work; in the film we can see the action taking place, the artist pouring his paint on the glass and controlling its movements with a stick. On the front of the glass, what Pollock described as 'coloured glass sheets and plaster slabs and beach stones and odds and ends of that sort' are encrusted into the paint; these enrich its colour and texture. But on the back there is another dimension; here we can see only the record of his movements, which were restless and unresolved but possessed a fundamental organic unity. As Pollock explained it in an interview with a neighbour in 1950, this work was intended to express 'an inner world – in other words expressing the energy, the motion and other inner forces'. He saw this as an antidote to the mechanical age in which he was living, and which, unlike Mondrian and Léger, he did not enjoy.

130

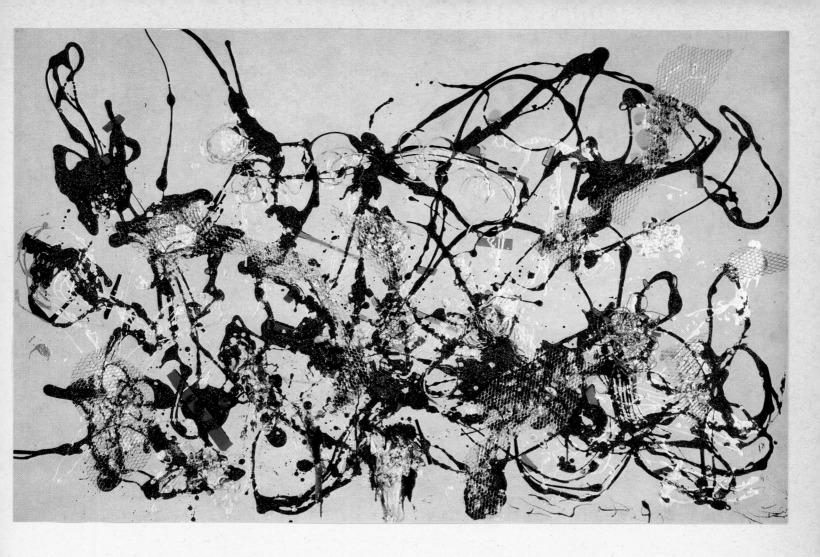

XXXII Paul Emile Borduas

Saint-Hilaire 1905 — Paris 1960

3 + 4 + 1, 1956

Oil on canvas, 78 x 98 in. (198.1 x 248.9 cm.)
No. 9858. Bought from the Martha Jackson Gallery, New York, 1962.

Behind this painting is a spiritual pilgrimage that may have begun when Ozias Leduc converted the fifteen-year old Borduas to painting as he decorated the village church in their native Saint-Hilaire. In any case, as Borduas said later, 'Dès mes premiers contacts avec Leduc, comme beaucoup d'autres, j'ai été séduit par sa simplicité.' Although Leduc's late murals were flat and decorative, the younger artist would have known earlier paintings like his *Still Life* (plate XXV) and respected the feeling for substance and texture that developed in his own work. Borduas has said: 'La peinture, la peinture physique, la matière, la pâte. C'est là mon sol natal, c'est ma terre.' And certainly we feel it here.

Borduas, who studied in Montreal and, during two years in Paris, with Maurice Denis briefly at his École d'Art Sacré, became in 1937 a teacher at the École du Meuble in Montreal. About 1940 he saw his first copy of the surrealist magazine, *Minotaure,* with poems by André Breton that affected him profoundly and drove him to his first abstract paintings two years later. At the same time he was teaching – a process in which he was constantly stimulated by his students to question his values. Much of what he absorbed was disturbingly contradictory and seemed to explode in an anarchistic manifesto of 1948 called *Refus global* that resulted in his dismissal from the École du Meuble. Five years later he went to New York ('où je me suis trouvé,' he said). There he would go to the Club, the informal centre of Abstract Expressionism, and talk with artists like Franz Kline and Robert Motherwell, who describes Borduas as the Courbet of the twentieth century.

In 1955 Borduas moved to Paris where the next year he painted this picture. An interview there revealed that he was conscious of two poles in his work: Mondrian, who to him was equating space with light, and Jackson Pollock, who was 'releasing his exasperation in paint'. Borduas was neither as disciplined as the one nor as uninhibited as the other but, like both, he strove for understanding as he plastered white paint on the large canvas with his palette knife and opened it up for patches like black water seen through snow-covered ice – three, plus four, plus one.

132

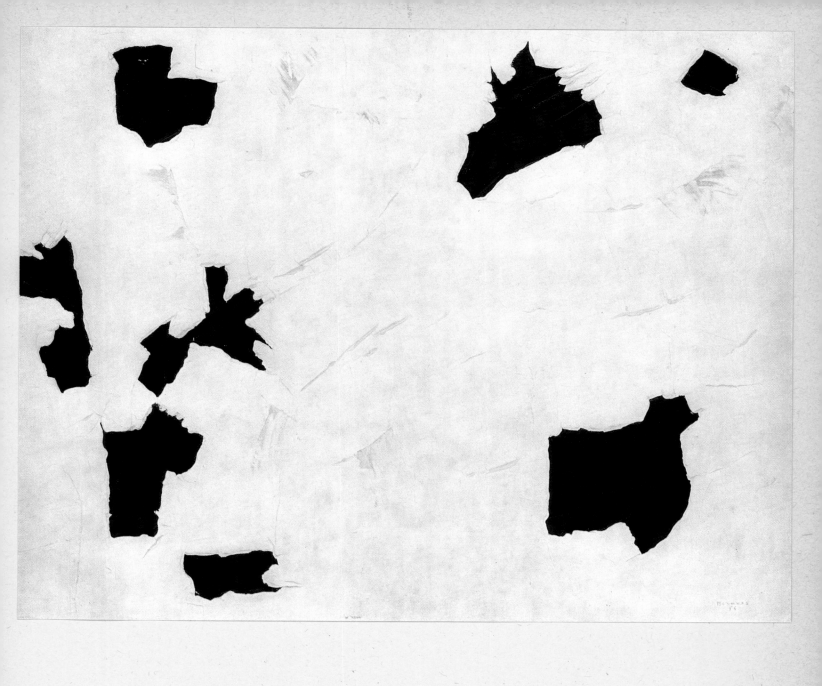

Index of Artists

Figures refer to plate numbers

1 FRENCH GOTHIC, 15th century
Madonna and Child
Limestone with traces of colour, $43\frac{1}{2}$ in. high
(110.5 cm.).
No. 6487. Bought 1956.

2 NERI DI BICCI, Florence, 1419–c. 1491
The Assumption of the Virgin, by 1454
Tempera on panel, 85 × 87 in. (215.9 × 221.0 cm.).
No. 3716. Bought 1930.

3 BENOZZO GOZZOLI, Florence, *c.* 1421–1497
Madonna and Child with Saints, 1473?
Tempera on panel, 61 × 62 in. (154.9 × 157.5 cm.).
No. 6084. Bought 1952.

6 FLEMISH SCHOOL, 16th century
Portrait of a Canon
Oil on panel, 41 × 35 in. (104.2 × 88.9 cm.).
No. 3701. Gift of H. S. Southam, Ottawa, 1930.

5

4   FILIPPINO LIPPI, Florence, 1457/8–1504
     The Triumph of Mordecai, c. 1474–80
     Tempera on panel, 19¼ × 17 in.
     (48.9 × 43.2 cm.).
     No. 6086. Bought 1953.

5   Studio of SANDRO BOTTICELLI (1444/5–1510),
     Florence
     Two Children
     Tempera on panel, 14½ × 10 in.
     (36.8 × 25.4 cm.).
     No. 3524. Bought 1927.

4

7

7 BARTEL BRUYN the Elder, Cologne, 1493–1555
Portrait of Elisabeth von Brauweiler, 1544
Oil on panel, $18\frac{1}{2} \times 13\frac{3}{4}$in. (47.0 × 35.9 cm.).
No. 732. Bought 1913.

8 LUCAS CRANACH the Elder, Saxony, 1472–1553
Venus
Oil on panel, 68 × 27 in. (172.7 × 68.6 cm.).
No. 6087. Bought 1953.

9 School of GIOVANNI BELLINI (*c.* 1430–1516), Venice
Standing Christ
Tempera on canvas transferred from panel, $62\frac{3}{4} \times 35$ in.
(159.4 × 88.9 cm.).
No. 328. Bought 1912.

10 BARTOLOMEO MONTAGNA, Vicenza, *c.* 1450–1523
St Jerome
Oil on canvas transferred from panel, $40\frac{5}{8} \times 53\frac{3}{4}$ in.
(103.2 × 136.5 cm.).
No. 3699. Bought 1929.

9

10

12

11

11 VINCENZO CATENA, Venice, c. 1480–1531
The Holy Family in a Landscape, c. 1525
Oil on canvas, $33\frac{1}{2} \times 52\frac{1}{2}$ in. (85.1×133.4 cm.).
No. 9586. Bought 1961.

12 DOSSO DOSSI, Ferrara, c. 1490–1542
Aeneas at the Entrance of the Elysian Fields, c. 1520–1
Oil on canvas, $22\frac{1}{2} \times 65\frac{3}{4}$ in. (57.2×167.0 cm.).
No. 14666. Bought 1964.

13 BERNARDINO LUINI, Milan, c. 1480/5?–1532
The Christ Child and St John with a Lamb
Oil on canvas transferred from panel, $31 \times 22\frac{5}{8}$ in.
(78.8×57.5 cm.).
No. 3454. Bought 1927.

14 GIOVANNI CARIANI, Venice, *fl.* 1509–1547
Portrait of a Man, c. 1520–40
Oil on canvas, $36\frac{1}{2} \times 36\frac{1}{2}$ in. (92.7×92.7 cm.).
No. 3568. Bought 1928.

13

14

15

15 TIZIANO VECELLIO called TITIAN, Venice, 1477?–1576
Portrait of Daniele Barbaro, 1545
Oil on canvas, $33\frac{3}{4} \times 28$ in. (85.8 × 71.1 cm.).
No. 3567. Bought 1928.

16 JACOPO ROBUSTI called TINTORETTO, Venice, 1518–1594
Portrait of a Man called Tintoretto's Servant
Oil on canvas, $42\frac{1}{4} \times 35$ in. (107.3 × 88.9 cm.).
No. 3453. Bought 1927.

17 PAOLO CALIARI called VERONESE, Venice, 1528?–1588
The Rest on the Flight into Egypt, c. 1560–70
Oil on canvas, 65 × 104 in. (165.1 × 264.2 cm.).
No. 4268. Bought 1936.

17

18 GIOVANNI FRANCESCO BARBIERI called IL GUERCINO, Bologna, 1591–1666
Christ and the Woman of Samaria, c. 1648?
Oil on canvas, 46×61$\frac{3}{8}$ in. (91.5×155.9 cm.).
No. 14809. Bought 1965.

19 ANDREA SACCHI, Rome, 1599–1661
Portrait of a Cardinal, c. 1630
Oil on canvas, 51 × 38 in. (129.5 × 96.5 cm.).
No. 305. Bought 1911.

20 LUCA GIORDANO, Naples, 1632/34–1705
The Crucifixion of St Andrew
Oil on canvas, 57 × 77 in. (144.8 × 195.6 cm.).
No. 4294. Gift of J. W. McConnell, Esq.,
Montreal, 1937.

19

20

22

21

23

21 ABRAHAM BLOEMAERT, Netherlands, 1564–1651
The Baptism of Christ, 1602
Oil on canvas, 23¾ × 30¼ in. (60.3 × 76.8 cm.).
No. 3340. Bought 1925.

22 ANTHONY VAN DYCK, Flanders, 1599–1641
Christ Blessing the Children, c. 1618
Oil on canvas, 51½ × 78½ in. (130.8 × 199.4 cm.).
No. 4293. Bought 1938.

23 JACOB JORDAENS, Flanders, 1593–1678
Young Cavalier Executing a Passade in the Presence of Mercury and Mars, c. 1645
Oil on canvas, 37¹³⁄₁₆ × 61½ in. (96.1 × 156.2 cm.).
No. 14810. Bought 1965.

24 REMBRANDT VAN RIJN, Netherlands, 1606–1669
The Tribute Money, 1629
Oil on wood panel, $16\frac{3}{4} \times 12\frac{7}{8}$ in. (42.5 × 32.7 cm.).
No. 15231. Bought 1967.

25 JAN LIEVENS, Netherlands, 1607–1674
Job, 1631
Oil on canvas, $67\frac{1}{2} \times 58\frac{1}{2}$ in. (171.5 × 148.6 cm.).
No. 4093. Gift of the National Art Collections Fund,
Great Britain, 1933.

26 MATTHIAS STOMER, Netherlands, *c.* 1600– after 1650
The Arrest of Christ
Oil on canvas, $61 \times 81\frac{1}{4}$ in. (154.9 × 206.4 cm.).
No. 4094. Bought 1933.

24

27 FRANS HALS, Netherlands, 1581/3–1666
Portrait of a Seated Man, *c.* 1645
Oil on panel, $16\frac{11}{16} \times 13\frac{1}{16}$ in. (42.4 × 33.2 cm.).
No. 15901. Bought 1970.

28 NICOLAES MAES, Netherlands, 1634–1693
The Lace-maker, 1655
Oil on panel, $22 \times 17\frac{1}{2}$ in. (55.9 × 44.5 cm.).
No. 6189. Bought 1954.

29 SALOMON VAN RUYSDAEL, Netherlands, 1600?–1670
River Landscape, 165(7?)
Oil on canvas, $38\frac{3}{8} \times 57\frac{7}{8}$ in. (97.5 × 147.0 cm.).
No. 3698. Bought 1930.

30 JAN STEEN, Netherlands, 1626–1679
The Lean Kitchen
Oil on panel, $27\frac{1}{2} \times 36\frac{1}{8}$ in. (69.9 × 91.8 cm.).
No. 9014. Bought 1960.

28

29

27

30

31 MEINDERT HOBBEMA, Netherlands, 1638–1709
Two Water-mills, after 1668
Oil on canvas, $35\frac{1}{2} \times 50\frac{1}{2}$ in. (90.2 × 128.3 cm.).
Gift of Queen Juliana of the Netherlands to the people of Canada, 1950.

32

33

32 SIMON VOUET, France, 1590–1649
The Fortune Teller, c. 1620
Oil on canvas, 47¼×67 in. (120.0×170.2 cm.).
No. 6737. Bought 1957.

33 CLAUDE LORRAIN, France, 1600–1682
A Temple of Bacchus, 1644
Oil on canvas, 37½×48 in. (95.3×121.9 cm.).
No. 4422. Bought 1939.

34

35

36

37

34 CHARLES LE BRUN, France, 1619–1690
Hercules and the Centaurs, c. 1650–5
Oil on canvas, $30\frac{1}{2} \times 44$ in. (77.5×111.8 cm.).
No. 4311. Bought 1938.

35 NICOLAS POUSSIN, France, 1594–1665
Landscape with a Woman Bathing, 1650?
Oil on canvas, 45×69 in. (114.3×175.3 cm.).
No. 4587. Gift of H. S. Southam, Ottawa, 1944.

36 DOMENICOS THEOTOCOPOULOS called EL GRECO, Spain, 1541–1614
St Francis in Meditation, with Brother Leo, before 1606
Oil on canvas, $66 \times 40\frac{5}{8}$ in. (167.7×103.2 cm.).
No. 4267. Bought 1936.

37 JUSEPE LEONARDO, Spain, *c.* 1605–1656
St John the Baptist, c. 1635–42
Oil on canvas, 60×44 in. (152.4×111.8 cm.).
No. 4292. Bought 1938.

38

38 ANTONIO CANAL called CANALETTO, Venice, 1697–1768
The Portals of St Mark's, Venice, by 1735
Oil on canvas, 52 × 65 in. (132.1 × 165.1 cm.).
No. 3718. Bought 1930.

39 BERNARDO BELLOTTO called CANALETTO, Venice, 1720–1780
The Arsenal at Venice, 1740–2
Oil on canvas, 59½ × 48 in. (151.1 × 121.9 cm.).
No. 3719. Bought 1930.

39

40 FRANCESCO GUARDI, Venice, 1712–1793
The Church of Santa Maria della Salute, Venice, 1780s
Oil on canvas, 28 × 37⅜ in. (71.1 × 94.9 cm.).
No. 6188. Bought 1954.

41 JEAN–BAPTISTE–SIMEON
CHARDIN, France, 1699–1779
La Pourvoyeuse, 1738
Oil on canvas, $18\frac{3}{8} \times 14\frac{3}{4}$ in.
(46.7 × 37.5 cm.).
No. 6433. Bought 1956.

42 ANTONIO CANOVA, Italy,
1757–1822
Dancer, 1818–22
Marble, 68 in. high
(172.7 cm.).
No. 15443. Bought 1968.

42

43

45

43 CAMILLE COROT, France, 1796–1875
Le Pont de Narni, 1827
Oil on canvas, $26\frac{3}{4} \times 37\frac{1}{4}$ in.
(68.0×94.6 cm.).
No. 4526. Bought 1940.

44 JEAN-FRANÇOIS MILLET, France,
1814–1875
Oedipe détaché de l'arbre, 1847
Oil on canvas, $52\frac{1}{2} \times 20\frac{1}{2}$ in.
(133.4×52.1 cm.).
No. 822. Bought 1914.

45 GUSTAVE COURBET, France, 1819–1877
Les Cascades
Oil on canvas, $38\frac{1}{2} \times 59\frac{1}{2}$ in.
(97.8×151.1 cm.).
No. 4638. Gift in memory of
Gordon C. Edwards, Ottawa, 1950.

44

46

47

46 ALFRED SISLEY, France, 1839–1899
Les Côteaux de Bougival, 1875
Oil on canvas, $19\frac{3}{4} \times 23\frac{1}{2}$ in.
(50.2 × 59.7 cm.).
No. 6094. Bought 1953.

47 CAMILLE PISSARRO, France, 1831–1903
Rue à l'Hermitage, à Pontoise, 1875
Oil on canvas, 23 × 36 in.
(58.4 × 91.5 cm.).
No. 4634. Bought 1946.

48 CAMILLE PISSARRO, France, 1831–1903
*Le pont de pierre à Rouen, temps
gris*, 1896
Oil on canvas, 26 × 36 in.
(66.0 × 91.5 cm.).
No. 2892. Bought 1923.

49 CLAUDE MONET, France, 1840–1926
*Waterloo Bridge: le soleil dans le
brouillard*, 1903
Oil on canvas, $27\frac{1}{2} \times 38\frac{1}{2}$ in.
(69.9 × 97.8 cm.).
No. 817. Bought 1914.

48

49

No. 5770. Bought 1950.

54 EDGAR DEGAS, France, 1834–1917
Portrait of a Woman (after Pontormo), *c.* 1858
Oil on canvas, $25\frac{1}{2} \times 17\frac{7}{8}$ in. (64.8 × 45.4 cm.).
No. 15222. Bought 1966.

55 EDGAR DEGAS, France, 1834–1917
Danseuses à la barre, *c.* 1900
Pastel on paper, $43\frac{1}{4} \times 37$ in. (109.9 × 94.0 cm.).
No. 1826. Bought 1921.

56 PIERRE-AUGUSTE RENOIR, France, 1841–1919
Claude et Renée, 1903
Oil on canvas, 31 × 25 in. (87.7 × 63.5 cm.).
No. 4989. Bought 1949.

57 PAUL GAUGUIN, France, 1848–1903
Portrait Head of Meyer de Haan, 1889–90
Wood with touches of colour, 23 in. high (58.4 cm.).
No. 15310. Bought 1968.

58 ANDRE DERAIN, France, 1880–1954
*Paysage au bord de la mer: la Côte
d'Azur près Agay*, 1905
Oil on canvas, 21 × 25 in.
(53.3 × 63.5 cm.).
No. 5880. Bought 1952.

59 GEORGES BRAQUE, France,
1882–1963
Le Port d'Anvers, 1906
Oil on canvas, 19⅝ × 24 in.
(49.8 × 61.0 cm.).
No. 5782. Bought 1951.

60 GEORGES ROUAULT, France, 1871–1958
Les deux filles, 1906
Watercolour with pastel,
$27\frac{1}{2} \times 21\frac{1}{2}$ in. (69.9 × 54.6 cm.).
No. 15267. Bought 1967.

61 KEES VAN DONGEN, Netherlands
and France, 1877–1968
*Souvenir de la saison de l'Opéra
russe*, 1909
Oil on canvas, $21\frac{1}{4} \times 25\frac{1}{2}$ in.
(54.0 × 64.8 cm.).
No. 14984. Bought 1966.

62 LYUBOV SERGEIEVNA POPOVA, Russia and France, 1889–1924
The Pianist, c. 1916
Oil on canvas, 42×35 in. (106.7×88.9 cm.).
No. 14930. Bought 1966.

63 JACQUES LIPCHITZ, Lithuania and France, 1891–
Seated Figure, 1917
Limestone, 30 in. high (76.2 cm.).
No. 6426. Bought 1955.

64

64 PABLO PICASSO, Spain and France, 1881–
 Le guéridon, 1919
 Oil on canvas, $45\frac{3}{4} \times 28\frac{3}{4}$ in. (116.2 × 73.0 cm.).
 No. 6768. Bought 1957.

65 HENRI MATISSE, France, 1869–1954
 Nu au canapé jaune, 1926
 Oil on canvas, $21\frac{1}{4} \times 32$ in. (54.0 × 81.3 cm.).
 No. 6971. Bought 1958.

65

66 CORNELIUS JOHNSON, England, 1593–1661
Portrait of Lady Thynne, 1636
Oil on canvas, 31 × 25¼ in. (78.7 × 64.1 cm.).
No. 7008. Gift in memory of Paul Oppé, 1958.

67 WILLIAM HOGARTH, England, 1697–1764
Portrait of John Herring, 1740
Oil on canvas, 29 × 24 in. (73.7 × 61.0 cm.).
No. 295. Bought 1911.

69 THOMAS GAINSBOROUGH, England, 1727–1788
Portrait of Ignatius Sancho, 1768
Oil on canvas, 29 × 24½ in. (73.7 × 62.2 cm.).
No. 58. Bought 1907.

68 SIR JOSHUA REYNOLDS, England, 1723–1792
Portrait of Charles Churchill, 1755
Oil on canvas, 47½ × 38 in. (120.7 × 96.5 cm.).
No. 29. Bought 1910.

71 GEORGE ROMNEY, England, 1734–1802
Portrait of Joseph Brant, 1776
Oil on canvas, 50×40 in. (127.0×101.6 cm.).
No. 8005. Bought 1918.

70 RICHARD WILSON, England, 1714–1782
A Distant View of Rome from Monte Mario, before
1765
Oil on canvas, 39½×53¼ in. (100.3×135.3 cm.).
No. 4879. Bought 1948.

72 JAMES PHILIP DE LOUTHERBOURG, France and England, 1740–1812
A Midsummer Afternoon with a Methodist Preacher, 1777
Oil on canvas, 38 × 49¾ in. (96.5 × 126.4 cm.).
No. 4057. Bought 1932.

73

73 SIR HENRY RAEBURN, Scotland, 1756–1823
Portrait of Jacobina Copland, c. 1794
Oil on canvas, $30 \times 25\frac{1}{4}$ in. (76.2×64.1 cm.).
No. 9928. Bought 1962.

74 RICHARD PARKES BONINGTON, England, 1802–1828
Landscape with a Wagon, 1825
Oil on canvas, $14\frac{1}{2} \times 20$ in. (36.8×50.8 cm.).
No. 3457. Bought 1926.

74

75 J. M. W. TURNER, England, 1775–1851
The Shipwreck
Oil on canvas, 46 × 56¼ in. (116.9 × 142.9 cm.).
No. 3455. Bought 1926.

77

76 ABRAHAM SOLOMON, England, 1824–1862
First Class Meeting . . . and at First Meeting Loved, 1854
Oil on canvas, $27\frac{1}{4} \times 38\frac{1}{8}$ in. (69.2 × 96.9 cm.).
No. 14667. Bought 1964.

77 WILLIAM HOLMAN HUNT, England, 1827–1910
Portrait of Henry Wentworth Monk, 1858
Oil on canvas, 20 × 26 in. (50.8 × 66.0 cm.).
No. 39. Bought 1911.

78 DANTE GABRIEL ROSSETTI, England, 1828–1882
Salutatio Beatricis, 1859
Oil on panel, each panel $29\frac{1}{2} \times 31\frac{1}{2}$ in. (74.9 × 80.0 cm.).
No. 6750. Bought 1957.

78

76

81

79

79 LORD LEIGHTON, England, 1830–1896
Sansone, c. 1882?
Oil on canvas, 10×7 in. (25.4×17.8 cm.).
No. 369. Gift of the artist, 1883.

80 SIR JOHN EVERETT MILLAIS, England, 1829–1896
Portrait of the Marquis of Lorne
Oil on canvas, 40×29 in. (101.6×74.0 cm.).
No. 82. Gift of the artist, 1884.

81 GEORGE FREDERICK WATTS, England, 1817–1904
Time, Death, and Judgment, 1882 or earlier
Oil on canvas, 96×65½ in. (243.9×166.4 cm.).
No. 130. Gift of the artist, 1887.

82 WALTER RICHARD SICKERT, England, 1860–1942
*The Old Bedford, c.*1890
Oil on canvas, 50×30½ in. (127.0×77.5 cm.).
No. 4810. Gift of the Massey Foundation, 1946.

80

83 WALTER RICHARD SICKERT, England, 1860–1942
Rue Notre-Dame, Dieppe, 1902
Oil on canvas, 52 × 41⅝ in. (132.1 × 105.7 cm.).
No. 4809. Gift of the Massey Foundation, 1946.

84 JAMES MCNEILL WHISTLER, United States and England,
1834–1903
Lillie in Our Alley (The Lady of Lyme Regis), c. 1898
Oil on canvas, 20½ × 12½ in. (52.1 × 31.8 cm.).
No. 4628. Bought 1946.

85 WALTER GREAVES, England, 1846–1930
Milman Street, Chelsea
Oil on canvas, 33½ × 43½ in. (85.1 × 110.5 cm.).
No. 353. Bought 1912.

84

85

86

86 SIR JACOB EPSTEIN, United States and England, 1880–1959
Rock Drill, 1913–14
Bronze, 28 in. high (71.1 cm.).
No. 6498. Bought 1956.

87 HAROLD GILMAN, England, 1876–1919
Halifax Harbour at Sunset, 1918
Oil on canvas, 77 × 132 in. (195.6 × 335.2 cm.).
No. 8172. Deposited 1921.
The War Collections

88 PAUL NASH, England, 1889–1946
Void, 1918
Oil on canvas, 28 × 36⅛ in. (71.1 × 91.7 cm.).
No. 8650. Deposited 1921.
The War Collections

89 EDWARD WADSWORTH, England, 1889–1949
Dazzle-ships in Drydock at Liverpool
Oil on canvas, 119½ × 96 in. (303.5 × 243.8 cm.).
No. 8925. Deposited 1921.
The War Collections

87

89

88

90 HENRY MOORE, England, 1898–
Reclining Woman, 1930
Stone, 36 in. long (91.4 cm.).
No. 6499. Bought 1956.

91 STANLEY SPENCER, England, 1891–
Landscape with Magnolia, Odney Club, 1938
Oil on canvas, $36\frac{1}{8} \times 24\frac{1}{8}$ in. (91.8 × 61.3 cm.).
No. 4817. Gift of the Massey Foundation, 1946.

92 FRANCIS BACON, England, 1910
Study for Portrait, No. 7, 1956
Oil on canvas, $77\frac{1}{2} \times 55\frac{3}{4}$ in.
(196.9 × 141.6 cm.).
No. 6746. Bought 1957.

92

90

93 HENRY BENBRIDGE, United States, 1743–1812
The Tannatt Family
Oil on canvas, 39 × 64½ in. (99.1 × 163.8 cm.).
No. 9003. Gift of Jasper H. Nicolls, Ottawa, 1960.

94 ROBERT HENRI, United States, 1865–1929
Portrait of George Luks, 1904
Oil on canvas, 76½ × 38¼ in. (194.3 × 97.2 cm.).
No. 9587. Bought 1961.

95 ARTHUR DOVE, United States, 1880–1946
Rising Tide, 1944
Oil on canvas, 27¼ × 36¼ in. (69.2 × 92.1 cm.).
No. 15721. Gift of Mrs E. F. Eidlitz, St Andrews, N. B., 1968.

96 LYONEL FEININGER, United States and Germany, 1871–1956
Yachts, 1950
Oil on canvas, 21 × 36 in. (53.3 × 91.5 cm.).
No. 15719. Gift of Mrs E. F. Eidlitz, St Andrews, N. B., 1968.

94

93

95

96

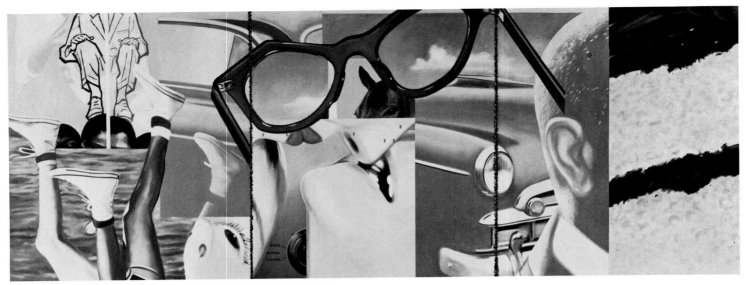

97

98

99

97 JAMES ROSENQUIST, United States, 1933–
For the American Negro, 1962–3
Oil on canvas, 80×210 in. (203.2×533.4 cm.).
No. 15292. Bought 1967.

98 DAVID SMITH, United States, 1906–1965
Wagon I, 1963–4
Painted steel, $88\frac{1}{2} \times 121\frac{1}{2} \times 64$ in. (224.8×308.6×162.5 cm.).
No. 15703. Bought 1968.

99 GEORGE SEGAL, United States, 1926–
The Gas Station, 1963
Assemblage, 8.6×24.2×4 ft. (259.1×736.6×121.9 cm.).
No. 15560. Bought 1968.

101

100 FRANÇOIS-NOEL LEVASSEUR, Canada, 1703–1794
Kneeling Angel
Wood, 20⅛ in. high (51.1 cm.).
No. 7792. Bought 1960.

101 FRANÇOIS BEAUCOURT, Canada, 1740–1794
Self-portrait, c. 1770
Oil on canvas, 13½ × 10½ in. (34.3 × 26.7 cm.).
No. 4354. Bought 1939.

102 THOMAS DAVIES, England and Canada, active 1755–1812
A View of the Casionchiagon or Great Seneca Falls, Lake Ontario, 1766
Watercolour, 13⅜ × 20¼ in. (34.0 × 51.4 cm.).
No. 6273. Bought 1957.

103 ANONYMOUS, active Quebec early 19th century
The Esplanade, Quebec, c. 1818
Watercolour, 12¹³⁄₁₆ × 16¹¹⁄₁₆ in. (32.6 × 42.4 cm.).
No. 16627. Bought 1971.

100

102

103

105

106

104 SALOMON MARION, Canada, 1782–1830
Madonna
Silver, 19⅞ in. high (base excluded) (50.5 cm.).
No. 9669. Gift of E. E. Poole, Edmonton, 1962.

105 ANONYMOUS, Canadian 19th century
Portrait of Mrs Charles Morrison, c. 1825–30
Oil on canvas, 26 × 22¼ in. (66.1 × 56.5 cm.).
No. 9008. Bought 1960.

106 THEOPHILE HAMEL, Canada, 1817–1870
Portrait of Madame Guay, 1841
Oil on canvas, 33 × 28 in. (83.9 × 71.1 cm.).
No. 6981. Bought 1958.

107 ROBERT C. TODD, Canada, active 1834–1865
The Ice Cone, Montmorency Falls, c. 1845
Oil on canvas, 13½ × 18 in. (34.3 × 45.7 cm.).
No. 6763. Bought 1957.

108 PAUL KANE, Canada, 1810–1871
Blackfoot Chief and Subordinates, 1851–6
Oil on canvas, 25 × 30 in. (63.5 × 76.2 cm.).
No. 22. Transferred from Parliament, 1888.

104

107

108

109

111

110

109 CORNELIUS KRIEGHOFF, Europe and Canada, 1815–1872
       Owl's Head, Memphremagog, 1859
       Oil on canvas, $17\frac{1}{4} \times 24$ in. (43.8×61.1 cm.).
       No. 15490. Bequest of Vincent Massey, 1968.

110 WILLIAM RAPHAEL, Germany and Canada, 1833–1914
       Bonsecours Market, Montreal, 1866
       Oil on canvas, $26\frac{1}{2} \times 43$ in. (67.4×109.2 cm.).
       No. 6673. Bought 1957.

111 ANTOINE PLAMONDON, Canada, 1804–1895
       Still Life with Apples and Grapes, c.1870
       Oil on canvas, $27\frac{1}{2} \times 30\frac{1}{4}$ in. (69.9×76.8 cm.).
       No. 108. Transferred from Parliament, 1888.

112

112 HOMER WATSON, Canada,
1855–1936
The Laurentides, 1882
Oil on canvas, $25\frac{1}{2} \times 41\frac{1}{2}$ in.
(64.8 × 105.4 cm.).
No. 122. Deposited 1883.
R.C.A. Diploma
Collection

113 WILLIAM BRYMNER, Canada,
1855–1925
A Wreath of Flowers, 1884
Oil on canvas, $47\frac{1}{2} \times 55$ in.
(120.6 × 139.7 cm.).
No. 19. Deposited 1886.
R.C.A. Diploma
Collection

114 ROBERT HARRIS, Canada,
1849–1919
Harmony, *c*. 1888
Oil on panel, $12 \times 9\frac{3}{4}$ in.
30.5 × 24.8 cm.).
No. 6757. Bought 1957.

113

117

118

115 PAUL PEEL, Canada, 1860–1892
A Venetian Bather, 1889
Oil on canvas, 61½ × 44½ in. (156.2 × 113.0 cm.).
No. 17. Bought 1895.

116 GEORGE AGNEW REID, Canada, 1860–1947
Mortgaging the Homestead, 1890
Oil on canvas, 50½ × 83½ in. (128.3 × 212.1 cm.).
No. 86. Deposited 1891.
R.C.A. Diploma Collection

117 OZIAS LEDUC, Canada, 1864–1955
L'Enfant au pain, 1892–9
Oil on canvas, 19⅞ × 22 in. (50.5 × 55.9 cm.).
No. 15793. Bought 1969.

118 HORATIO WALKER, Canada, 1858–1938
Oxen Drinking
Oil on canvas, 47½ × 35½ in. (120.7 × 90.2 cm.).
No. 300. Bought 1911.

119 LOUIS PHILIPPE HEBERT, Canada, 1850–1917
L'Inspiration, 1904
Bronze, 22½ in. high (57.2 cm.).
No. 245. Deposited 1907.
R.C.A. Diploma Collection

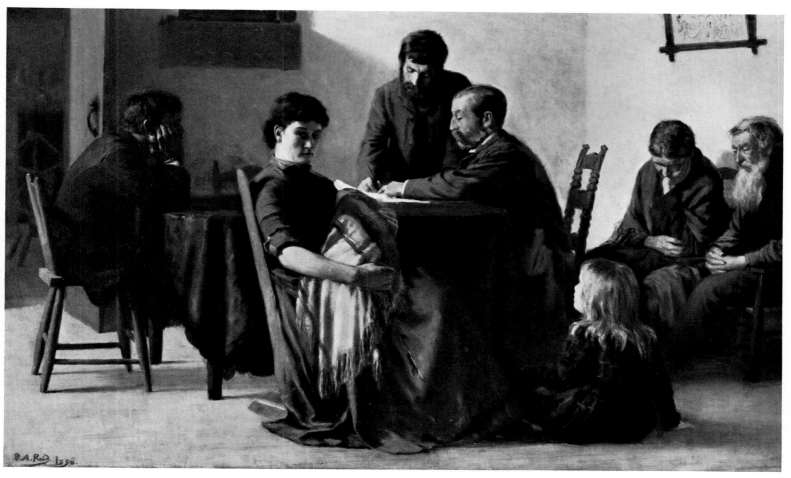

120

120 JAMES WILSON MORRICE, Canada and France,
1865–1924
Quai des Grands-Augustins, Paris, c. 1903
Oil on canvas, 19¼ × 23½ in. (48.9 × 59.7 cm.).
No. 73. Bought 1909.

121 JAMES WILSON MORRICE, Canada and France,
1865–1924
Olympia, c. 1912
Oil on canvas, 32 × 24 in. (81.3 × 61.0 cm.).
No. 6671. Bought 1957.

122 MAURICE CULLEN, Canada, 1866–1934
The Ice Harvest, c. 1906
Oil on canvas, 29½ × 39½ in. (74.9 × 100.3 cm.).
No. 740. Bought 1913.

123 CLARENCE A. GAGNON, Canada, 1881–1942
Village in the Laurentian Mountains
Oil on canvas, 34½ × 51 in. (87.6 × 129.5 cm.).
No. 3529. Bought 1927.

122

123

EMILY CARR

126 TOM THOMSON, Canada, 1877–1917
Snow in October, 1914–16
Oil on canvas, $32\frac{1}{4} \times 34\frac{1}{4}$ in. (81.9×88.3 cm.).
No. 4722. Bequest of Dr James MacCallum,
1948.

125 EMILY CARR, Canada, 1871–1945
Forest Landscape (I)
Oil on paper, 36×24 in. (91.4×61.0 cm.).
No. 5041. Bought 1950.

124 EMILY CARR, Canada, 1871–1945
Tanoo, c. 1912
Watercolour, $29\frac{3}{4} \times 21$ in. (75.6×53.3 cm.).
No. 3542. Bought 1928.

124

126

127 A. Y. JACKSON, Canada, 1882–
   The Red Maple, 1914
   Oil on canvas, $31\frac{1}{4} \times 38\frac{1}{4}$ in. (79.4 × 97.1 cm.).
   No. 1038. Bought 1914.

128 A.Y. JACKSON, Canada, 1882–
Houses of Ypres, 1917
Oil on canvas, $25 \times 30\frac{1}{4}$ in.
$(63.5 \times 76.9$ cm.).
No. 8207. Deposited 1921.
The War Collections

129 J.E.H. MACDONALD, Canada,
1873–1932
The Tangled Garden, 1916
Oil on board, 48×60 in.
$(121.9 \times 152.4$ cm.).
No. 4291. Presented in memory
of Richard Southam by his
brothers, 1939.

130 F.H. VARLEY, Canada, 1881–1969
Some Day the People Will Return, 1918
Oil on canvas, 72 × 90 in. (182.9 × 228.6 cm.).
No. 8910. Deposited 1921.
The War Collections

131 F.H. VARLEY, Canada, 1881–1969
Stormy Weather, Georgian Bay, c. 1920
Oil on canvas, 52×64 in. (132.1 × 162.6 cm.).
No. 1814. Bought 1921.

133

132 F.H. VARLEY, Canada, 1881–1969
Vera, c. 1930
Oil on canvas, 24 × 20 in.
(61.0 × 50.8 cm.).
No. 15559. Bequest of Vincent Massey,
1968.

133 ARTHUR LISMER, Canada, 1885–1969
A September Gale, Georgian Bay, 1921
Oil on canvas, 48 × 64 in.
(121.9 × 162.6 cm.).
No. 3360. Bought 1926.

134 LAWREN HARRIS, Canada, 1885–1970
January Thaw, Edge of Town, 1921
Oil on canvas, 42 × 50 in.
(106.7 × 127.0 cm.).
No. 5005. Gift of the artist, 1950.

134

135

135 LAWREN HARRIS, Canada, 1885–1970
Lake Superior III, c. 1928
Oil on canvas, $34\frac{1}{2} \times 40\frac{1}{4}$ in. (87.6×102.2 cm.).
No. 15477. Bequest of Vincent Massey, 1968.

136 LAWREN HARRIS, Canada, 1885–1970
Equations in Space, c. 1936
Oil on canvas, 30×48 in. (76.2×121.9 cm.).
No. 15673. Bought 1968.

137 BERTRAM BROOKER, Canada, 1888–1955
Alléluiah, c. 1929
Oil on canvas, $48\frac{1}{8} \times 48$ in. (122.2×121.9 cm.).
No. 15812. Bought 1969.

138 EMANUEL HAHN, Canada, 1881–1957
Head of Elizabeth Wyn Wood, 1926
Marble, 23 in. high (58.4 cm.).
No. 3545. Bought 1928.

138

137

136

139 DAVID MILNE, Canada, 1882–1953
Painting Place, 1930
Oil on canvas, $20\frac{1}{4} \times 26\frac{1}{4}$ in. (51.4×66.7 cm.).
No. 15520. Bequest of Vincent Massey, 1968.

140 L. L. FITZGERALD, Canada, 1890–1956
Doc Snider's House, 1931
Oil on canvas, $29\frac{1}{2} \times 33\frac{1}{2}$ in. (74.9×85.1 cm.).
No. 3993. Gift of Dr P. D. Ross, Ottawa, 1932.

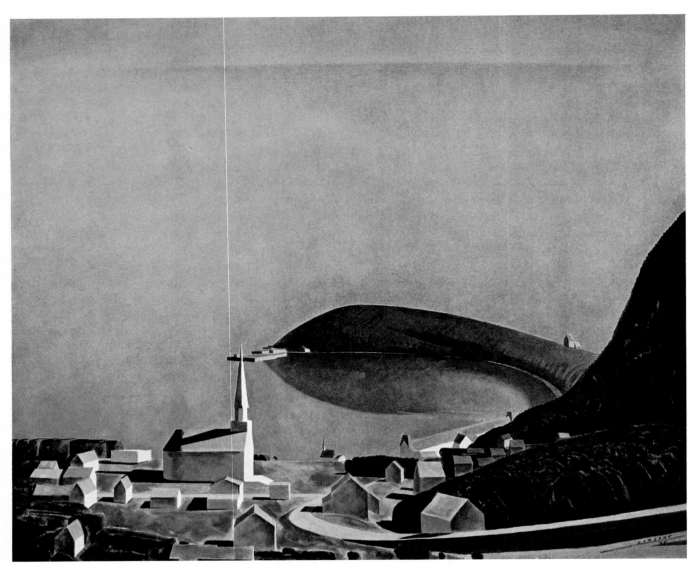

141 CHARLES COMFORT, Canada, 1900–
Tadoussac, 1935
Oil on canvas, 30×36 in. (76.2×91.5 cm.).
No. 15471. Bequest of Vincent Massey, 1968.

142 GOODRIDGE ROBERTS, Canada, 1904–
Landscape near Lake Orford, September 1945
Watercolour, $21\frac{1}{4} \times 29\frac{1}{2}$ in. (54.0×74.9 cm.).
No. 4867. Bought 1948.

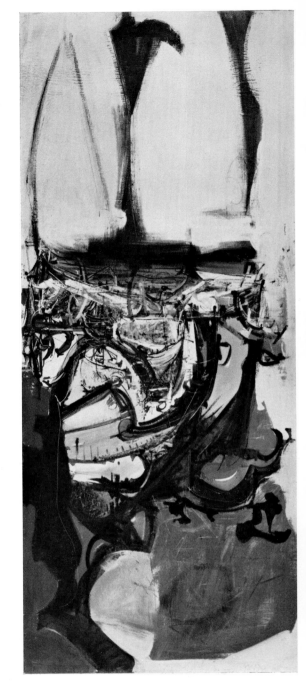

145

144

146

143 ALFRED PELLAN, Canada, 1906–
Sur la plage, c. 1953
Oil on canvas, 81¾×66 in. (206.7×167.7 cm.).
No. 9512. Bought 1961.

144 JEAN-PAUL RIOPELLE, Canada, 1923–
La Roue, No. 2
Oil on canvas, 78½×78½ in. (199.4×199.4 cm.).
No. 6691. Bought 1957.

145 HAROLD TOWN, Canada, 1924–
Dead Boat Pond, 1956
Oil on canvas, 95½×38 in. (242.6×96.5 cm.).
No. 6695. Bought 1957.

146 GUIDO MOLINARI, Canada, 1933–
Angle noir, 1956
Oil on canvas, 60×72 in. (152.4×182.9 cm.).
No. 15236. Bought 1967.

143

147 JEAN-PAUL LEMIEUX, Canada, 1904–
Le Train de midi, 1956
Oil on canvas, $24\frac{3}{4} \times 43\frac{1}{2}$ in. (62.9 × 110.5 cm.).
No. 6913. Bought 1957.

148 ALEX COLVILLE, Canada, 1920–
Hound in Field, 1958
Casein tempera on board, 30×40 in. (76.2×101.6 cm.).
No. 7163. Bought 1959.

149

150

151

149 ALEX COLVILLE, Canada, 1920–
To Prince Edward Island, 1965
Acrylic polymer emulsion on board, $24\frac{1}{2}\times 36\frac{1}{2}$ in. (62.2 × 92.7 cm.).
No. 14954. Bought 1966.

150 GREG CURNOE, Canada, 1936–
The Camouflaged Piano or French Roundels, 1965–6
Oil and damar on wood, $98\frac{1}{4}\times 146\frac{1}{2}$ in.
(249.6 × 372.1 cm.) (with lighting attachment).
No. 14975. Bought 1966.

151 JACK BUSH, Canada, 1909–
Tall Spread, 1966
Acrylic polymer on canvas, $107\times 50\frac{1}{4}$ in. (271.8 × 127.6 cm.).
No. 14974. Bought 1966.

152 CLAUDE TOUSIGNANT, Canada, 1932–
Gong 88, No. 1, 1966
Liquitex on canvas, 88 in. diameter (223.5 cm.).
No. 15260. Bought 1967.

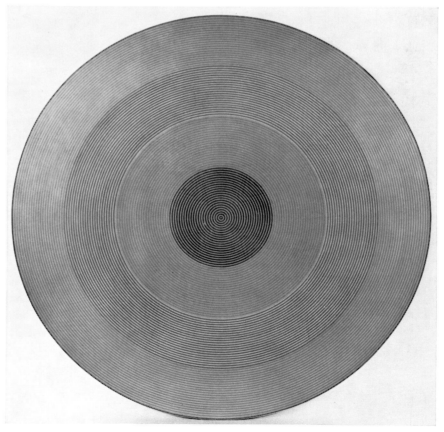

152

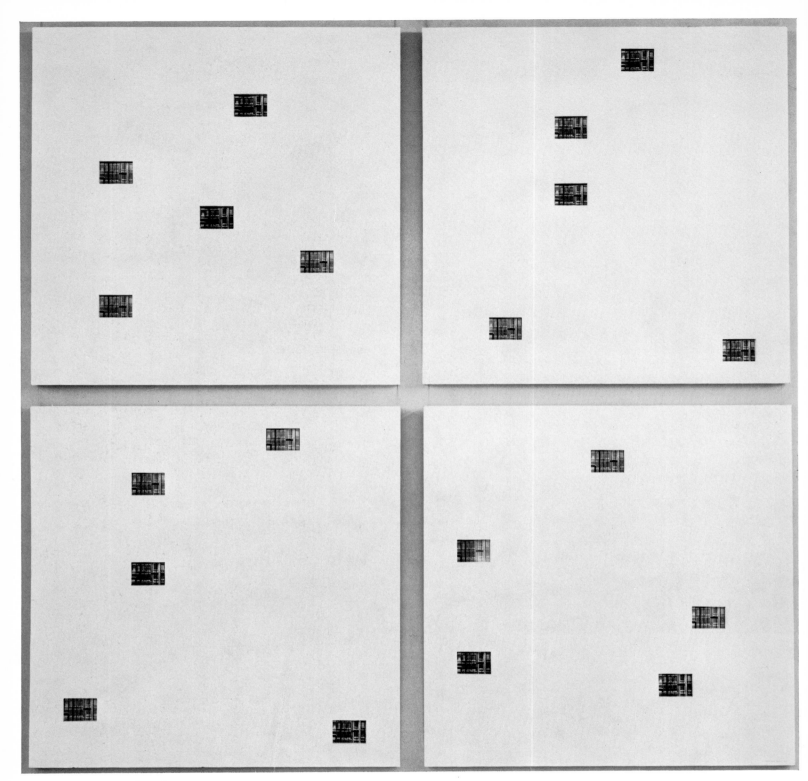

153 MICHAEL SNOW, Canada, 1929–
Snow-Storm, February 8, 1967
Photograph and enamel on masonite, 4 panels, 48 × 47 in. each (121.9 × 119.4 cm.).
No. 15456. Bought 1968.

154 ULYSSE COMTOIS, Canada, 1931–
Column, 1967–8
Aluminium, 77 × 64 in. (195.6 × 162.6 cm.).
No. 15261. Bought 1968.

155 ROBERT MURRAY, Canada, 1936–
Breaker, 1965
Painted aluminium, $47\frac{1}{4}$ × 114 × $57\frac{1}{8}$ in.
(120.0 × 289.6 × 145.1 cm.).
No. 15321. Bought 1967.

154

155

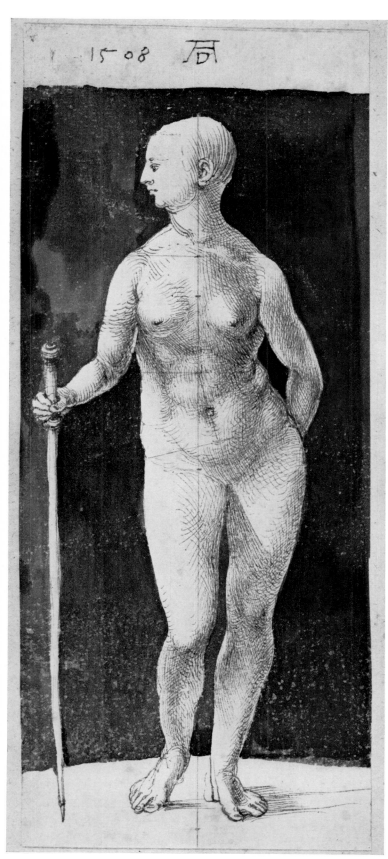

157

156 ITALIAN SCHOOL, 15th century
Nine Famous Men, c. 1450
Pen and brown ink with watercolour on parchment,
$12\frac{5}{16} \times 7\frac{11}{16}$ in. (31.4×19.6 cm.).
No. 9896. Bought 1962.

157 RAPHAEL, Italy, 1483–1520
Youthful Saint, c. 1502–3
Metalpoint on prepared cream-coloured paper; laid down,
$4\frac{13}{16} \times 1\frac{15}{16}$ in. (12.2×4.9 cm.).
No. 5085. Bought 1939.

158 ALBRECHT DURER, Germany, 1471–1528
Nude Woman with a Staff
Pen and wash, $9\frac{1}{4} \times 3\frac{3}{4}$ in. (23.5×9.6 cm.).
No. 6652. Gift of Joseph Hirshhorn, Esq., and a group of his
friends and associates, 1956.

159

161

160

163

162

159 JACOPO BASSANO, Italy, 1510/15–1592
The Presentation of the Virgin, 1569
Coloured chalks on blue-grey paper, $20\frac{1}{4} \times 14\frac{7}{8}$ in. (51.6 × 37.8 cm.).
No. 4431. Bought 1938.

160 HANS BOL, Netherlands, 1534–1593
The Bird Catchers I, 1582
Pen and wash, $2\frac{11}{16} \times 8\frac{5}{8}$ in. (6.9 × 21.9 cm.).
No. 4554. Bought 1940.

161 JACQUES BELLANGE, France, 1594–1638
St John the Baptist Preaching
Black chalk and wash, $11\frac{7}{8} \times 12\frac{9}{16}$ in. (30.1 × 31.9 cm.).
No. 15770. Bought 1968.

162 ANNIBALE CARRACCI, Italy, 1560–1609
The Lute-player and Other Studies, c. 1590
Pen, ink and wash on pale green paper, $11\frac{1}{4} \times 9\frac{1}{8}$ in. (28.6 × 23.1 cm.).
No. 279. Bought 1911.

163 PETER PAUL RUBENS, Flanders, 1577–1640
Study of a Young Man's Head
Black chalk on buff paper, $12\frac{5}{16} \times 11$ in. (31.3 × 28.0 cm.).
No. 6159. Bought 1953.

164 ANTOINE WATTEAU, France, 1684–1721
Two Male Figures Standing
Red chalk, $6\frac{15}{16} \times 7\frac{7}{16}$ (17.7 × 18.9 cm.).
No. 4548. Bought 1939.

165 FRANÇOIS BOUCHER, France, 1703–1770
An Angel Bringing Food to a Hermit
Black chalk, $12\frac{7}{16} \times 8\frac{1}{2}$ in.
(31.6×21.6 cm.).
No. 6888. Gift of Mrs Samuel Bronfman,
Montreal, 1957.

166 GIOVANNI BATTISTA PIRANESI, Italy,
1720–1778
Fantastic Interior, c. 1750
Pen and ink and wash over red chalk,
$4\frac{7}{8} \times 7\frac{1}{16}$ in. (12.4×18 cm.).
No. 4993. Bought 1948.

165

166

168 FRANCISCO GOYA, Spain, 1746–1828
A Young Witch Swinging, c. 1826
Black chalk, $7\frac{1}{2} \times 6\frac{1}{8}$ in. (19.2 × 15.5 cm.).
No. 2996. Bought 1923.

169

167 GIOVANNI DOMENICO TIEPOLO, Italy, 1727–1804
Visiting Time at a Nunnery, 1791
Pen and ink and washes over black chalk,
$11\frac{5}{16} \times 16\frac{3}{8}$ in. (28.8 × 41.6 cm.).
No. 15349. Bought 1967.

169 FRANCISCO GOYA, Spain, 1746–1828
Holy Week in Spain in Past Times, c. 1825
Black chalk, $7\frac{1}{2} \times 5\frac{3}{4}$ in. (19.2 × 14.7 cm.).
No. 2999. Bought 1923.

167

170

171

170 EUGÈNE DELACROIX, France, 1798–1863
    The Crucifixion, c. 1846–52
    Pastel on grey paper, $9\frac{1}{2} \times 6\frac{11}{16}$ in. (24.1 × 17.0 cm.).
    No. 15733. Bought 1968.

171 GUSTAVE MOREAU, France, 1826–1898
    Hésiode et la muse, 1858
    Pen and brown ink over black chalk heightened with white and ink on beige paper, $14\frac{13}{16} \times 11\frac{7}{16}$ in.
    (37.7 × 29.0 cm.).
    No. 15213. Bought 1966.

172 HONORÉ DAUMIER, France, 1808–1879
    À l'audience or *Three Judges at a Hearing*
    Pen and ink and grey wash over black chalk, $5\frac{1}{4} \times 9\frac{7}{8}$ in. (13.3 × 25.0 cm.).
    No. 812. Bought 1914.

173 VINCENT VAN GOGH, Netherlands and France, 1853–1890
    The Swamp, 1881
    Pen and ink over graphite on cream paper, $18\frac{3}{8} \times 23\frac{5}{16}$ in. (46.8 × 59.3 cm.).
    No. 15461. Bought 1967.

172

173

174 ODILON REDON, France, 1840–1916
The Raven, 1882
Charcoal, $15\frac{3}{4} \times 11$ in. (40.0 × 27.9 cm.).
No. 14847. Bought 1965.

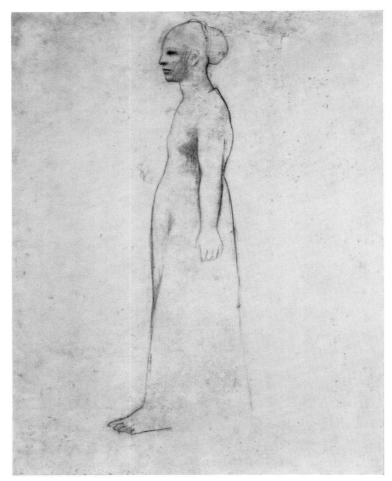

175 PABLO PICASSO, Spain and France, 1881–
Young Woman Standing in Profile to the Left, 1906
Black chalk, $24\frac{5}{16} \times 18\frac{7}{16}$ in. (61.8 × 46.8 cm.).
No. 6222. Bought 1953.

176 ERNST LUDWIG KIRCHNER, Germany, 1880–1938
Portrait of a Woman, c. 1906
India ink wash and watercolour, $17\frac{5}{8} \times 14\frac{1}{16}$ in. (44.8 × 35.7 cm.).
No. 9844. Bought 1962.

177 ALBERT MARQUET, France, 1875–1947
Nude, c. 1910–12
Brush and black ink, $12\frac{1}{16} \times 8\frac{3}{4}$ in. (30.6 × 22.2 cm.).
No. 6705. Bought 1956.

178

179

178 ERICH HECKEL, Germany, 1883–1970
Portrait of the Artist's Wife, 1913
Charcoal, watercolour and gouache with touches of graphite, $19\frac{11}{16} \times 16\frac{1}{16}$ in. (50.1 × 40.8 cm.).
No. 15269. Bought 1967.

179 PAUL KLEE, Germany and Switzerland, 1879–1940
Fox 1926
Pen and ink and wash, $8\frac{15}{16} \times 6\frac{3}{8}$ in. (22.7 × 16.2 cm.).
No. 6635. Bought 1956.

180 HENRI MATISSE, France, 1869–1954
Dancer Resting in an Armchair, 1939
Charcoal, $25\frac{1}{4} \times 18\frac{13}{16}$ in. (64.0 × 47.7 cm.).
No. 15355. Bought 1967.

181

182

183

184

181 GEORGE ROMNEY, England, 1734–1802
Dido Bidding Farewell to Aeneas (?), *c.* 1773–5(?)
Brush and wash over chalk, $10\frac{15}{16} \times 16\frac{1}{4}$ in. (27.8 × 41.2 cm.).
No. 9069. Bought 1960.

182 SAMUEL PALMER, England, 1805–1881
Old Oak Tree, Shoreham, Kent, c. 1828
Pen and ink and gouache on grey paper, $11\frac{5}{8} \times 18\frac{3}{8}$ in. (29.5 × 46.7 cm.).
No. 4357. Bought 1937.

183 SIR JOHN EVERETT MILLAIS, England, 1829–1896
The Return of the Dove to the Ark, 1851
Pen and ink and grey wash, $9\frac{3}{16} \times 5\frac{1}{16}$ in. (23.3 × 12.9 cm.).
No. 14661. Bought 1964.

184 AUGUSTUS JOHN, England, 1878–1961
Dorelia in a Black Hat, c. 1909–12
Black chalk and grey wash, 14 × 10 in. (35.7 × 25.4 cm.).
No. 9890. Bought 1962.

185 CH'IU YING, China, 1st half of the 16th century
The Emperor Kuang Wu Fording a River
Ink and colour on silk, 67¼ × 25¾ in.
No. 6485. Bought 1956.